CALLED TO BE
AMISH

PL△INSPOKEN
Real-life stories of Amish and Mennonites

ADVANCE PRAISE FOR *CALLED TO BE AMISH*:

"Marlene C. Miller did what few folks have successfully done: left the English world and its conveniences and married an Amish man. In her book, readers will marvel at the power of love. What began as earthly love blossoms into a love for God, family, and Amish living."
—*Paul Stutzman, author of* Hiking Through *and* Biking Across America

"For someone who came from a non-Amish culture to write a book about being Amish is quite remarkable. This book will give you insights about the Amish culture because the writer has had decades of real-life experience. It gives details about Amish life that you may not find in any other book on the market."
—*Anne Beiler, founder of Auntie Anne's, Inc.*

"A rare treat! Marlene C. Miller converted to the Amish after she became a Christian, and her story chronicles her journey of faith and family. Written by a delightful woman, this enjoyable read will overturn many of your perceptions about the Amish."
—*Suzanne Woods Fisher, best-selling author of Amish fiction and nonfiction*

CALLED TO BE
AMISH

*My Journey from Head Majorette
to the Old Order*

MARLENE C. MILLER

Herald Press
Harrisonburg, Virginia
Kitchener, Ontario

Library of Congress Cataloging-in-Publication Data
Miller, Marlene C., 1944-
[Grace leads me home]
Called to be Amish : my journey from head majorette to the Old Order / Marlene C. Miller.
pages cm. -- (Plainspoken : Real-Life Stories of Amish and Mennonites)
"Released simultaneously in Canada by Herald Press, Kitchener, Ontario"--Title page verso.
"An earlier version of this book was self-published by the author and entitled Grace Leads Me Home : From Head Majorette to Old Order Amish"--Title page verso.
ISBN 978-0-8361-9911-6 (pbk. : alk. paper) 1. Miller, Marlene C., 1944-
2. Amish women--Ohio--Biography. 3. Amish--Ohio--Biography. 4. Miller, Marlene C., 1944---Marriage. 5. Miller, Marlene C., 1944---Family. 6. Conversion--Christianity. 7. Amish--Ohio--Social life and customs. 8. Teenage girls--Ohio--Stark County--Biography. 9. Drum majorettes--Ohio--Stark County--Biography.
10. Stark County (Ohio)--Biography. I. Title.
F500.M45M56 2015
289.7092--dc23
[B]

2014033758

CALLED TO BE AMISH
© 2015 by Herald Press, Harrisonburg, Virginia 22802. 800-245-7894.
All rights reserved.
Library of Congress Control Number: 2014033758
International Standard Book Number: 978-0-8361-9911-6
Printed in United States of America
Cover and interior design by Merrill Miller
Cover photo by Merrill Miller

Photos used throughout this book are from the author's collection.

An earlier version of this book was self-published by the author and entitled *Grace Leads Me Home: From Head Majorette to Old Order Amish* (Sugarcreek, OH: Carlisle Printing, 2011).

Unless otherwise noted, Scripture text is quoted with permission from the *King James Version.*

19 18 17   10 9 8 7 6 5 4

I dedicate this book first and foremost to God's Son, Jesus Christ. Without his cross and his blood, there would be no Savior.

Second, I dedicate this book to my loving and patient husband, John. He is one of the finest people I have ever known, and I consider it an honor and blessing to be his wife.

CONTENTS

INTRODUCTION TO

PL△INSPOKEN
Real-life stories of Amish and Mennonites

AMISH NOVELS, Amish tourist sites, and Amish-themed TV shows offer second- or third-hand accounts of Amish and Mennonite life. Some of these messages are sensitive and accurate. Some are not. Many are flat-out wrong.

Now readers can listen directly to the voices of the Amish themselves through Plainspoken: Real-Life Stories of Amish and Mennonites. In the books in this series, readers get to hear Amish and Mennonite writers talk about the texture of their daily lives: how they spend their time, what they value, what makes them laugh, and how they summon strength from their Christian faith and community.

The Amish are publishing their writing more than ever before. In periodicals like *Die Botschaft* and the *Budget*, Amish writers across Canada and the United States connect with each other. Amish printing presses and publishing houses bring books by Amish authors to Amish readers. But such magazines and books are read mostly by other Amish and Mennonites and rarely by the larger reading public.

Until now. Now readers can learn what authentic Amish life looks and feels like—from the inside out. The Amish and Mennonites have stories to tell. Through Plainspoken, readers get the chance to hear them.

Author's Note

I'D LIKE TO THANK Elsie Kline for typing my first draft. Because I wrote everything longhand, I'm sure she had a very difficult time.

I want to express another hearty thank-you to Cathy McCrea of Meridian, Idaho. She worked faithfully for a year, writing, rewriting, and editing. She pulled many more memories from my brain so, as she would say, she could expand on the stories. She was a joy to work with, and an absolute Godsend. I also want to thank her husband, Russ, for the patience he displayed and the meals he prepared while she typed.

I want to thank the hundreds of people who encouraged me to write my English-to-Amish story. A thank-you also to Wanda E. Brunstetter, Charlotte Thompson, and to my nine living children and forty-one grandchildren.

I had no idea it would take four years from start to finish, but the Lord's timing, not mine, is forever perfect. I give all the praise and glory to God. Amen.

—*Marlene C. Miller*

Part I

1

Prayers for a Blue-Eyed Girl

STANDING IN THE bathroom and getting dressed for my wedding on an April morning, I felt an anxious dread deep in my stomach. When someone knocked at the door, I went through the kitchen to the living room, thinking it was Johnny coming to pick us up and take us to the church for our wedding. Instead it was Clara, my friend who was to be the maid of honor.

My whole family was in final preparations for this wedding, which I had planned for and waited for so long. As I walked back into the bathroom to finish dressing, I could see the silent looks of anxiety on the faces of my parents. Dad stood in front of the mirror in the kitchen, combing his hair, while Mom, Greg, and Clara waited nearby.

I put on my stockings and shoes and had just pulled on my dress, starting to zip it, when the phone rang. My hand on the zipper froze, and I ran to my brother Franny's bedroom to answer the phone, my dress flapping at the back. Everyone could hear the conversation, as Franny's bedroom was right off the living room. I just knew in my gut that it was going to be Johnny.

"Hello," I slowly spoke into the receiver. When I heard Johnny's voice I was very scared. In my heart I knew what was coming, but I dreaded it all the same.

"Marlene, I can't marry you."

My heart stopped. The whole world stopped.

"You just can't do this to me, Johnny. You just can't do this to me. Can you honestly tell me you don't love me? Can you? Tell me!"

He answered, "I've got to go now. Bye." The connection went dead.

Franny came into his room but never said a word, which was unusual for him. I staggered out of the room and collapsed on the couch. My parents ran to me, demanding, "Was that Johnny?"

I looked up, willing my eyes to focus, and finally answered, "Yes. He said he won't marry me." The preparations ceased in that instant. I saw shock freeze the faces of Clara and Franny, who were standing nearby, waiting to attend at the wedding. My parents were the first to react, knowing the wedding guests were already at the church and had to be told the wedding was off.

"Marlene, you stay put and don't go anywhere," they ordered. "After we go tell the people at the church that the wedding is off, we will go to see Johnny's parents!" And out they flew.

I went back upstairs, my body going through the motions of taking off my wedding dress. It seemed I was moving in a fog. I couldn't believe this was happening to me. All the dreams and plans I had fostered for so long were cut off the moment the phone line went dead. The pain in my stomach, and in my heart, was as real and as sharp as if someone had punched me. All the years of time and events in my life met together at this sharp point of focus.

How had it all come down to this?

Looking in from the outside, our small-town life in Beach City, Ohio, must have seemed idyllic. But it's unbelievable what went on behind closed doors in our little town, in our little family.

On a cold, blustery day in February 1944, I was born to Ronald Wynford Bailey and Margaret Frances Smith Bailey at Massillon City Hospital, weighing six pounds and measuring eighteen inches. I was named Marlene Carol Bailey after the famous actress Marlene Dietrich, as Mom later told me.

My first recollection of home is our eight-room house with a dirt-floored basement, an oil stove for heat, an icebox for food, a crank telephone, and a coal-and-wood stove for cooking. We loved when the iceman came in the heat of the summer. There wasn't anything better than when he gave us a big piece of ice, which we would wrap in a clean washcloth and suck on for a cool treat. It was our poor man's Popsicle, cold and yummy— minus the stick and the flavoring!

Marlene, age one, outside her family's home in Beach City.

I had three older brothers—Larry Ronald, Garry Donald, and Francis Allen—plus a brother ten years younger than me, Gregory Leland. My mother's parents said my parents were elated to have a blond, blue-eyed girl after having three rowdy boys.

Right from the beginning I believe God had his hand on me. My mom hired an Amish girl to come in for six weeks, as the custom was to have help after having a baby. Years later I found out this girl was my husband's first cousin, Sarah Yoder. I have a feeling she may have prayed for me in those weeks she lived with us.

Often I didn't like my mom and dad, as it seemed they were always swearing, or angry, or hitting us for what seemed like no reason. I was too young to realize it then, but I see now that they must have been very unhappy with themselves and they didn't know Jesus. What I experienced later in life showed me that a person must have Jesus in his or her life to be truly happy.

There was precious little physical affection in our family, and I can only remember my dad hugging me one time. We were at the Buckeye Beagle Club, where my dad often took his dogs to train. A man was talking with my dad, and he asked, "Is this your daughter?"

When my dad raised his hand, I subconsciously flinched and thought, *Look out. He's going to hit me.* Instead, my dad pulled me to him, smiled, and said, "Yes, this is my only daughter." From the cradle in his arm, I looked up at him and felt special at that moment. For once in my life I had a brief feeling of approval from my dad.

My dad and his dad before him raised beagle dogs. This was the passion of their lives, where they spent their time and

Marlene's father, Ronald Bailey, with one of the many beagles he raised and one of trophies he won.

money. Dad had at least thirty dogs, including puppies, most of the time, and the biggest part of his money went to vet bills, dog food, and going to the field trials. Dad worked eight hours a day in a steel mill, and the only time he missed work was when a piece of steel flew into his leg, which caused him to be off work for a year. Every few weeks, Dad laid one hundred dollars on the corner of the kitchen table for Mom to use for house payments, groceries, electricity, gas, and water. There was precious little left over for anything else, and we learned early on not to ask for much.

Marlene's grandpa Lemuel Smith (*seated*), with her aunt Velda Miller (*middle*) and grandmother Jennie Smith.

Thank God for my grandparents and aunts who must have prayed for me; they had a big impact on my life. My mom's parents were Jennie and Lemuel Smith. My aunts and uncles were Aunt Velda and Uncle Howard Miller, Aunt Grace and Uncle Charles Goepfert (whom we called Chuck), and Great-Aunt Idella, who never married. I loved Aunt Velda and wished she had been my mom, because she was so kind and giving, just like my Grandma Smith.

My great-grandma Frances Baskey's image comes to my mind like a photograph, with her snow-white hair done up in a bun, wearing one of the dark dresses she always wore. She almost looked Amish, except she wore no *Kapp* (prayer covering) on her head. When I was about five, Mom worked with Franny and me so we could sing a song for Great-Grandma on our visit the next Sunday afternoon. Over and over we practiced the hymn "It Is No Secret (What God Can Do)." When the day came, there Grandma Baskey sat, a tiny little woman in her rocker, while Franny and I stood proudly before her, giving our little song. I felt honored to sing for her, and I remember how she smiled for our performance.

She died soon after this, and the viewing was in her living room. This was the first time I had seen a dead person, so I was a little afraid when I went to view her. I knew that people who died were usually taken to a funeral home, so having her laid out at home was different. I heard people saying how nice it was for her viewing to be at home. Little did I know then that I would be having a similar viewing in my Amish home many years later.

Aunt Grace and Uncle Chuck had one daughter, Charlene. I wore all her hand-me-down clothes until I got too plump to fit into them. She was tall and very, very slim. My body runs to the shorter, stouter side, so I wasn't very old before this arrangement no longer worked.

When I was five years old, my mom took me to a seamstress in our town to have some clothes made. Mrs. Hays was a plump older woman with gray hair and a pleasant face. How I loved the green wool jumper she made me, but I felt funny when she had me stand on her dining table to pin the hem. I had never stood on a table before. It certainly wouldn't have been tolerated at home. Each time she told me to turn as she pinned up the bottom of the skirt, Mrs. Hays was so kind and gentle that it made a lasting impression on me.

She and her husband had a very beautiful home with lovely woodwork and an open stairway. Maybe that's why I always

Marlene in second grade, wearing a green jumper made by Mrs. Hays.

wanted an open stairway. After twenty-four years of marriage, I finally got one. I loved going to the Hays' home because it was so peaceful, and they seemed such quiet and happy people. I never heard a swear word there. When my mom quit taking me there, I really felt like something was missing. I think back and wonder: were they praying for the little blue-eyed girl, too?

That same year, something wonderful happened that was to shape the direction of my life for many years: I started taking dance lessons. Each week my mom walked with me two houses past the schoolhouse to take tap, ballet, and acrobatics lessons in a converted garage. It seemed natural to me to dance, because I loved music and I really loved tap dancing. I have no idea where the money came from for these lessons, but it didn't matter to me. It opened up an exciting new world of music and movement that was delightful.

After I took lessons for a year or so, a group of us girls from the dance studio entered a talent contest held on the school-house stage. One of the mothers made our outfits: light pink dresses with white binding on the short sleeves and around the hem of the skirt. How cute we all looked and felt in those pretty dresses. I don't remember what place we won, but I was very happy when we won a prize. Right then, I knew I loved per-forming. The dancing and the music became a part of me.

I was in another talent contest during seventh grade with my friend Dorothy Nicsinger. We sang a duet together and again we won a prize, maybe second place. These early successes with performing surely were a factor in my desire, later on, to become a cheerleader and a majorette.

A loving companion joined my life during these early years. Mom said a little black puppy followed my brothers home from school one day. I loved that little puppy right from the start, and Blacky quickly became my pal. She lived with us for years until she died from a bad heart and arthritis.

Blacky and Marlene as a young girl.

Christmas was my favorite time of year, because Mom bought gifts and went all out for us during this holiday season. The year I was seven, we had the most people ever in our home for Christmas Eve: Uncle Chuck and Aunt Grace and their daughter, Charlene; Uncle Howard and Aunt Velda; and Grandpa and Grandma Smith. Our house was bursting at the seams, but I loved having all my favorite relatives there. It gave me a warm feeling of family and belonging.

Like every family, we had our traditional foods for the holiday. Grandma brought baked ham and buns so we could have sandwiches, and she always brought her beautiful, decorated cutout cookies. Her cookies were decorated with frosting colors that made sense to me—not like you might see now with blue animals and red trees. One of Grandma's cookie shapes was a chicken, which was decorated with yellow frosting. The trees were frosted green. I loved looking at them, but I guess I didn't look at them too long before I popped one in my mouth.

Earlier that year I had noticed a baby doll displayed for sale in the window of the local restaurant. What a lovely doll! The outstanding blue color of her dress and her eyes caught my attention and took my breath away. Every day as I walked home from school I stared and stared at her when I passed the restaurant. I wanted her so much I could almost taste her.

Then one day when I went past the window, she was gone. I couldn't believe it. My baby doll was gone! I went home crying my heart out. I had been telling Mom all about her, how lovely she was, and how much I wanted her, and now she was gone. I thought my heart would break.

Christmas Eve came and we opened our gifts. There were the usual pajamas from Grandma. To my memory Grandma never bought me a toy; it was either something to wear or something to eat. If she hadn't bought clothes for all of us children, I don't know what we would have had to wear. I don't ever remember my dad giving my mom money to buy us clothes or anything else specifically for us. We had food and shelter, but clothes were evidently not considered real necessities, so Grandma almost always bought our clothes. This made me sincerely thankful for those Christmas pajamas, and I loved her dearly for her caring.

Then I opened gifts from Aunt Grace and Aunt Velda. Having these gifts from the relatives I treasured made my heart glow, and sitting in this circle of happiness and love gave me a feeling of acceptance and belonging that I seldom felt at home.

When I opened the gift from Mom, I found my baby doll with the blue eyes and the blue dress; the one I had longed for was now my very own. I really, really loved her, and happy feelings for my mom welled up in me for surprising me with such a treasured gift.

Marlene at age seven (*center*), with the new doll she received for Christmas. *Clockwise, from bottom left,* Garry (brother), Franny (brother), Margaret (mother), Ronald (father), and Larry (brother). Charlene (cousin) sits at far right.

The Christmas I received my favorite baby doll was one of the happiest times of my childhood. The joy of those pleasant family times and playing with my doll still brings warmth into my heart as I think about it. Those happy times were like an oasis in a storm of often-troubled waters at our home.

Because Christmas was very important to Mom, this was one time she planned ahead to make sure it was special for all of us. She always bought our Christmas presents through the Sears Roebuck catalog. She had figured out how to manage money for these gifts, as she would pay for them by the layaway plan over one year, and then start over for the next. She did this for me year after year until I got married.

When Dad and Mom were getting along, I would hear Mom sing while she washed clothes or made dinner. During those times she smiled more, too. She was a very good singer and that must have been where I learned to love singing. Those were the happy times in our home. But when Dad went to field trials with his dogs in other states, he would be gone the entire weekend, which made her very sad and angry.

One Sunday afternoon when Dad was gone again, Mom and I were lying on the living room floor. She told me to take a nap, but I couldn't fall asleep right away. After a while when she thought I was asleep, I heard her crying. My heart ached as I lay there listening to her sob, but eventually sleep overcame me. When I awoke I looked at the clock, startled to see I had slept two hours. How eerie and sad it seemed as I woke to a kind of twilight darkness and a still house. The blinds were all pulled down on the windows toward the west, and the sun was

creeping in the sides and bottom of the blinds. As consciousness came over me, loneliness returned like a weight, hurting
deep in my body.

The aching feelings of that day with Mom stayed with me
as I grew up. Quiet Sunday afternoons were lonely in the years
before I met my husband. Sadness would often descend on
me again, pressing air out of my lungs. Even years after I had
become Amish, I didn't like the time of day around sunset, as
the emotional memories lingered in my heart like the slowly
dying sun.

Although my dad's parents lived only two houses away, I
didn't see them as much as I saw Grandpa and Grandma Smith,
who lived in the little town of Navarre. I had a special love for
Grandma and Grandpa Smith. I knew they truly loved me, with
no strings attached.

Marlene's great-grandparents, Ernest and Cecilia Welsh (*bottom row, center*), with their family. Marlene's paternal grandmother, Elsie, is in the back row, second from left.

My paternal grandma, Elsie Bailey, was kind and came from a loving, churchgoing family, but most of the time Grandpa Bailey was a mean person. Grandpa's parents were Catholic and had divorced when he was young. He was an only child and had a hard life growing up in Columbus. Many times he told me that children were to be seen and not heard, and he really meant it. When Grandma Bailey's relatives came to visit, we were invited over. I always went to visit, but Mom and Dad wouldn't go because of Grandpa Bailey's meanness. Dad said Grandpa had called him "the black sheep of the family."

My mom had her own reasons for the distance between them. She said Grandpa kicked my brother Garry's bottom very hard when he was a little boy. This made her so angry she said she "almost hated him and would never go over there again." I don't remember ever seeing her visit her in-laws.

From a young age I learned Grandpa Bailey's rules, and I was expected to respect and obey them all. When I visited I could talk only if I was asked a question. In those days we children were to sit in one chair during the entire visit and never move until we went home.

Once when Grandma Bailey had a bad heart condition and was ailing, I went to their house to iron for her. At that time everything was to be ironed. In our home, we ironed denims, work and dress shirts, pillowcases, dresses—everything. It seemed we had endless hours of ironing. Grandma's little amount of ironing was easy for me. It took me only an hour or so, because there wasn't that much. When I was finished she insisted on paying me, although I didn't want her to, and her generosity warmed my heart.

After I was married for about ten years, Grandpa Bailey gave us his butchering tools and big iron kettle. Since I was Amish and butchering hogs, he thought we could put the kettle to good use instead of putting flowers in it for a lawn ornament. He "didn't want anyone using it to plant flowers in." This was so like Grandpa. As an only child, he had learned to be independent, even to the point of controlling. However, when he was left alone after Grandma died, it seemed he had softened, and he cherished the times I would visit.

2

Longing for a Happy Family

IT WAS A drab, weary life at home during my early elementary years, with a mom who stayed in bed every morning. She got up, packed my dad's lunch, and made his oatmeal in the same aluminum pan all the years I was at home. But when it was time for us children to go to school, she was back in bed and yelled and yelled and yelled at us, telling us what to do or not to do that day. "Are you watching the clock, so you won't be late to school?" "Did you get your right clothes on?" "I heard the first bell ring for school; did you hear it?"

Every morning my oldest brother, Larry, made breakfast for the rest of us—cocoa and one loaf of bread made into toast—until he graduated. After that, it was up to me to take care of breakfast and supervise the morning chores. "Did you turn the burner off?" Mom would yell.

I wore pigtails in those days and had to bring the comb to Mom's bed, where I sat while she braided my hair. Years later, when I went to a friend's house to stay overnight, I learned that other mothers got up in the morning and helped their children to get fed and ready for school. That's when I realized there was something wrong with my mother.

A high point for me was when I stayed a week with Grandma Smith during the summer. She was always up bright and early and had the laundry on the line before eight o'clock in the morning on washdays. My mom never got up before ten o'clock, and washday was a terrible day for her, which made it a terrible day for all of us. I hated coming home from school on the day Mom washed. Even to this day I hate to smell bleach, because it reminds me of how angry Mom was on washdays and brings back memories of her complaining and mean looks. I didn't realize until I had my own family how hard she had to work to do the amount of laundry our family generated. Because the wringer-washer was in a room that had no drain, she had to carry buckets and buckets of water to and from the washer. Once the laundry was washed, she had the entire process to do over again, hauling more buckets of clean water, because she didn't have rinse tubs.

Laundry must have been doubly hard in the winter, when she had to hang the clothes on lines strung from window frame to window frame in the living room and into the kitchen. We had to fight through the clothes when we walked in the door or when we had supper. There are still nail holes in the woodwork of that house from where she hung those clotheslines. I never realized what a blessing it must have been to Mom when she finally got an automatic washer, with a gas clothes dryer soon after.

Mom was very particular about how the clothes were done, how they were sorted, and even how they were hung. When we hung the clothes outside, whites must only be hung with whites, colors with colors, and if we ever got it wrong, she chided, "What do you think the neighbors will think?"

Mom never allowed me to wash with the automatic washer, but I sneaked at it once when she was gone. When I was fourteen, I wore a sweater belonging to my brother Franny, who was four years older. He had told me when I borrowed it that I had to wash it before he would wear it again. I knew Mom used hot water on laundry days, so I thought that was how to wash everything. Unfortunately that sweater was made of wool, and when I took it out, my eyes almost popped out of my head! I pulled out this tiny, hard lump of wool that looked about size 4. When Franny saw his sweater, was he ever angry. Needless to say, I had to get rid of it, and I was "never, ever, and I mean *never*" to touch his clothes again. My washing days were over, except for washing my nylon hose by hand.

Although Mom was harsh with us at home, she had a kinder side that came out when my friends spent the night. A few times a year, one of my friends got to spend the night with me. They came home from school with me, ate supper, stayed the night, and went to school with me the next day. During those times, my mom put on a happy face and was very pleasant with these friends. She must have made good food for them, too, because one of my friends later remarked, "Your mom was a good cook."

———————

Mom's softer side, both her example and her words, also taught me to have compassion toward those less fortunate. A boy named Tom Hawkins lived across the alley behind us. Tom had a disability in his legs, feet, arms, and hands. He walked with his feet turned in, one hitting the other with each step. Walking must have been very difficult and painful for him, but he was very determined, and in spite of his disability he delivered newspapers to many people in town, including us. Tom's mom had a heart of gold, and I have never seen the equal of her patience with Tom. On collection day for the newspaper, she put change in Tom's pants pockets—bills in one pocket and coins in the other. If the customers didn't have the exact amount owed, they reached into his pockets to make their correct change.

Tom had a will of iron that was evident in his determination to peddle newspapers; he never gave up. His mother must never have given up either, because I'm sure the doctors told them he would never walk. It really impressed me that a person could overcome such tremendous odds, learn to be productive, and go on with his life.

Not only was Tom very industrious; he was also very smart. Many days we played checkers together. To move his checkers he sometimes used his hands or occasionally his toes, but most of the time he used his mouth. In all the hundreds of games I played with him, I never won. *Never.* He was so smart. At the end of the game, after winning again, he would laugh and laugh and say, "Maybe if we play again, you will win." And I was always gullible. Each time I truly believed that maybe I would win the next time, so I kept playing checkers with him.

Near the creek, down the alley from us, lived Debbie Agness, who was several years younger than me. She was born a beautiful, blond-haired, blue-eyed girl. But when Debbie was four or five, something happened to her, which I never did discover. From that time on, she couldn't walk and her eyes became crossed. She couldn't control her saliva and had to wear a bib. When her mother strolled through the alley with her, I often ran out to talk to Debbie a little. She couldn't really talk back, but I wanted somehow to show I really cared for her.

There was another little girl who lived across the street from us when I was about seven. I thought she was just a large baby, because her parents carried her everywhere. She was a beautiful child, and I wondered why she didn't stand up and walk because she was so big. At that young age, I didn't understand the mental and physical problems that some children have. To make her smile, I often went over to their house to hold rattles and toys for her. Then one day Mom announced very sadly that this girl had died and gone to heaven. I really felt badly that I would never see her again. Because I knew these special people from my childhood, I always feel pity for people who have mental or physical disabilities. Mom instilled in me the lesson that one must never tease or make fun of such children or adults.

On the same street where I lived, about three houses away, was an older man, Henry Shue. He was born with a huge elephant leg and seemed to have some mental impairment. But Henry also had a big heart. He was teased unmercifully at times, but I never teased him. I only felt pity for him. Henry responded to my kindness by showing his own care for me. He sometimes walked me home from uptown so that, in his words, "no one will get you."

Having friends like Henry to look after me helped me to feel very safe in our small town. I never had any fears at night walking home from school or activities. When I was younger my brothers sometimes walked with me, especially if it was at night. They often walked me from the skating bus to the beer joint where Mom worked. But from age ten I walked alone. Doors were never locked during the day in our town of about one thousand people. All we had on our door was a little slide lock that we locked at night.

I just found out people in big cities sometimes have up to three deadbolts and even chains on their doors. I have no idea what it would have been like to grow up having to lock yourself in and your neighbors out. To have to live behind locked doors would have been depressing to me. I surely would have lost some of the sense of security and carefree childhood that I enjoyed.

Early in my grade-school years our family got a little television, which we sat on an old library table in the living room. My brothers went together to buy this TV. They talked the dealer into giving them a loan so they could make payments. That little box opened up a world of wonder for me. The main programs I loved were Roy Rogers and Dale Evans and a circus program with a majorette doing her twirling act. I decided then and there that I wanted to twirl like her, because the twirling absolutely fascinated me. I also wanted a pony or a horse. At the end of each program Roy and Dale smiled and sang, "Happy trails to you, until we meet again." They looked into each other's eyes like they really loved each other. Those loving looks spoke to my heart. I didn't remember Mom and Dad ever looking at each other like that, but later on in my life I found those looks of love could happen for me. Sometimes dreams do come true.

One day I decided to go live with Roy and Dale, and I talked my little girlfriend Sue, who lived up the street, into running away with me. With the swearing, anger, lying, and cheating going on in our home, it was no surprise I wanted to live somewhere else. I wanted the peace and happiness that Roy and Dale radiated each time I saw their show, and I wanted a horse like

Trigger. I knew they had a special something, but at that time I didn't know much about the love of Christ, and how it could flow out of one person to touch another. I realize now that this must have been much of what drew me to them. It touches me to know the Rogers were Christians until they died.

With my mind made up to get a new family, I got out the suitcase my cousin had given me and packed it full. I was determined to gain peace and happiness, as well as a pony or a horse, that day. Sue and I went to the Greyhound bus stop at the drugstore in town and got on the bus. Often I had watched people get on the bus to go places, so I thought we could just walk on, tell the driver where we wanted to go, and he'd take us there. I didn't know we had to have a ticket to ride the bus. When the bus driver asked for our tickets, we were so surprised. We didn't have any tickets or money to buy them. Actually, we had no money at all to buy food or anything else we might need during our trip. I remember how kind the bus driver was when I told him we were going to live with the Rogers. He said very nicely, "When you have enough money to buy the ticket, you can go sometime." That day never came, and eventually the bus line quit coming to Beach City.

About the time I was nine years old, things got worse in our family life. We had a little more money because Mom had started working in the town tavern, but then the cheating started. And with the cheating came increased tension at home. Dad accused Mom of cheating, and she accused him. Mom worked Saturday nights, and I think she worked some nights during the week also. People told me my dad once threw a man out the door of this tavern because the man was "running his mouth off too much."

On Saturday nights while she worked, my mom sent my brothers and me on the bus to nearby New Philadelphia to the skating rink. After the rink closed around eleven o'clock, my brother Franny and I rode the bus back to Beach City and then walked to the tavern to stay until it closed. If we helped to clean up, we were paid by the owners. That was some of the first money I made as a girl. I liked being in the tavern because there were lots of people. It relieved the underlying loneliness for a while.

Plus there was the music. I loved listening to the jukebox. There were all kinds of songs—big band songs, polkas, and country songs from singers like Hank Williams and Grandpa Jones. I loved them all. This really increased my love of singing and music, which I have to this day.

My dad rarely drank. I only saw him drink a mixed drink on Christmas Eve and on New Year's Eve. Mom, on the other hand, loved to drink beer, and some nights she went with her women friends to taverns in nearby towns. Some of these women were married and some were widowed. When she took me along, sometimes I saw her flirt with other men. I suppose the other women did, too. This was very confusing and upsetting to me. I was only nine years old, and I couldn't figure out why, since she was married, she would do that.

If Grandma Smith had known about my mom's behavior, I'm sure she wouldn't have been happy with her. Grandma was full of Christian love and always encouraged me to go to church to learn about Jesus. She was a big influence on my soul. She listened to some preachers on TV and on Christian radio. Even though she didn't go to church, Grandma showed her love for Christ in her behavior and demeanor to me and to everyone around her. Every year, Grandma bought me a new outfit to wear on Easter so I would be sure to go to church.

I don't ever remember seeing my dad in church, but my mom took me to church one Christmas Eve so I could get candy and see Santa Claus coming down the aisle. My siblings and I usually went to church by ourselves. Although that was the only time I remember Mom taking me to church, one of my aunts recently told me, "I remember being at your house on a Saturday night when your mom had all your kids' shoes nicely polished with white polish, lined up on the warming shelf on her cookstove, ready for church the next day."

On Sundays when I heard the church bells ring, it bothered me if I didn't go to church. One day I asked Mom why she didn't go to church with me, and she said, "Church is for little children and old people, not for people my age." What an answer!

Something that influenced me and stayed with me for years was LaDean Byers's Good News Club. This gracious lady taught Bible stories to grade-school children in her home on Church Avenue—of all places. I went there with a group of friends after school and enjoyed these interesting stories. Mrs. Byers made Bible characters and themes come alive by using felt illustrations. She either ordered Bible characters or cut them out of heavy felt and placed them on a felt background. I learned more about the Bible there than from the times I went to Sunday school as a child.

The magical quality of the stories, as well as the musical part of these story times, drew me in. Mrs. Byers had a good friend who played the accordion during those story times. This friend played children's church songs while we all sang along. The polka programs I watched on TV also had accordion music. With only three channels on TV, that's about all there was to watch on Sunday afternoons. Because of this, I grew attached to the sound of the accordion, and for many years I longed for one. Years later, my husband bought me one at a sale.

My first cousin, Davy Eberhardt, was one of my playmates. We were the same age; I was born in February and he was born in August of the same year. Many times Davy and I, and sometimes my brothers, slept in Davy's tent in his backyard, which was right next door to our house. There was no fence between our homes. We often boxed and wrestled with each other because he had two pairs of boxing gloves. He always beat me in boxing, but I won the wrestling. He also had Lincoln Logs, which I loved to play with. We had hours and hours of fun with each other.

Marlene and her cousin Davy, both eight years old. Marlene is wearing her Roy Rogers cowboy boots.

Davy had a horse, which he kept in the backyard. As much as I wanted one, I never got a horse of my own, but I could ride his and did so often. There was no pasture, but his family had a little building out back that they used for a barn, where they fed him hay and grain. After about three or four years of this, the town made Davy pasture his horse out in the country. But so long as he was allowed this horse in town, we had many wonderful times riding. Davy must have enjoyed those times with his horse, too, because after going to Vietnam, he became a cowboy in California.

One of the brightest spots in my early childhood was my little friend Sue Wade, who had joined me in my plan to run away to live with Roy Rogers and Dale Evans. Sue lived four houses up the street from us, and she was an only girl in a family with three older brothers, just like me. The major difference between her family and mine was that I knew she was really loved. She didn't get whippings or beatings with a dog leash like we did. Sue's mother said, "I just don't know why your mother beats you." She often saw my mom beating me because our town park, where I often played, was across the street from their house. If I was playing basketball in the park with my brothers and didn't hear Mom call me to come home for supper or in the evening when it was curfew time, up the street my mom came, holding the leash behind her back and then beating me on my legs all the way home. I guess in those days people turned a blind eye to the way others disciplined their kids.

I wonder if my mom somehow knew of Mrs. Wade's disapproval of her harsh discipline, because most of the time Mom wouldn't speak to Mrs. Wade. I would say, "Why don't you go up to talk to Mrs. Wade while I play with Sue?" She would reply, "No, I don't talk to that woman. You just go on alone."

I often begged to go play house and dress-up at Sue's house. I really loved it there, because those were happy, peaceful times. I never saw Mr. or Mrs. Wade strike Sue, and I knew I would have a time of peace in their home.

Then one day Sue was really sick and they took her to the hospital. I will never in my life forget when they told me what was wrong with her. It was called polio. She was put into an iron lung to help her breathe, but died a day and a half later. I never got to go to the hospital to say goodbye, which made me really sad, because Sue was my best friend. We had so much fun together, and it was just tragic that she was taken from me so suddenly. It seemed to me that she was here and then just suddenly gone. Sue was the second person in my life to die. She died when I was eight. Great-Grandma Baskey had died when I was five.

After Sue died, Mom became close friends with Thelma Wade for many years, until Thelma's death. I never did understand why she waited so long to befriend Thelma; it would have been so peaceful for all of us had they been friends while Sue lived.

I went to view Sue at the funeral home, and I had to look at her through a big window. No one was allowed in her room, because at the time they thought polio was contagious. When I saw her, I was surprised at her curly hair. Sue had always had very straight hair and I had wavy hair. When I saw her beautiful hair of curls, I thought it was just lovely. She was dressed in a very pretty pink silk or taffeta dress, and she looked just like an angel.

I'm sure it was only minutes I stood there, but it felt like hours because I couldn't stand to part with her. I loved her so dearly.

3

The Amish Ice-Skater

MOM EDGED HER head around the corner of the door-way between the living room and the kitchen, and whispered, "Ronald, don't you think that's enough now?" But my dad couldn't hear above the cracks of the dog leash he was using to beat me after he had pushed me onto the couch.

Over and over, his angry blows seared pain into my body, while the humiliation burned into my spirit. The thought kept running through my mind, *I'll hate him till the day I die.* And I hated my mom for her part in this traumatic event. My head was reeling as the beating went on and on. I lost count of the blows and even felt myself slipping toward unconsciousness.

Finally, he stood back, threw the leash on the floor, and stomped out the back door, yelling, "Get the h— on your bike and deliver your newspapers. *Now!*"

I was thirteen years old and had an afternoon paper route. Earlier that hot summer day, as I had reached our home, which was the fourth on my route of fifty-four customers, I had to go to the bathroom. I had hopped off my brother Franny's bike and had run to the outhouse at the end of the property. While I was in the outhouse, my youngest brother, Greg, had begun tearing newspapers out of the bike basket and throwing them all over the yard.

When I came out and saw the mess, I got really angry and started giving him a licking with my hand. Papers were everywhere! Greg was only three at the time, but I felt he should know better than to do something like that. Greg started screaming as Mom ran out the back door. She yelled to my dad, who was cleaning a dog pen near the outhouse. Dad marched right up the yard, grabbed my arm, and pushed me inside the back door, through the kitchen into the living room, and onto the couch. And that's when the hate started.

Afterward, tears streaming down my face, I went around the yard gathering papers, trying to put them back together while my little brother laughed at me. My legs had such welts and bruises that I couldn't begin to sit on the bike seat, so I had to pedal standing up. It took me a long time to deliver those papers, over an hour of pain and anger. On and on the rhythm of hate played through my mind, fueled with the rhythm of the wheels and the tossing of the papers: *I'll hate him forever, I'll hate him forever.* And interspersed with that: *I'll hate her forever.*

I vowed that would be the very last beating I'd ever get. From then on, I would fight back or run away.

With all the strife and jealousy at home, I turned to school activities in my teenage years. My life revolved around music, band, cheerleading, and being a majorette. I loved all these wonderful activities and loved the sense of belonging they gave me.

Ice-skating was also a passion for me. When I turned thirteen in February, I went skating at the Beach City Dam. On that cold day I trudged out in the snow for a good mile and a half to join the other kids who were ice-skating there.

As I was making my way around the ice, I noticed a very nice-looking eighteen-year-old Amish boy and his friends skating very well. This boy wasn't wearing Amish clothes, but I knew he was Amish because of his accent. He really impressed me. I thought he could skate like a pro because he could skate backward just as well as forward.

"Hey, would you teach me how to do that?" I asked. He took off, demonstrating some of his skating techniques, forward and backward, and especially making beautiful circles going backward. I took off trying to skate just as he had done, thinking I was copying his techniques.

"No," he said, "you're crossing your feet over the wrong way. Don't pick up your foot so much; just let it flow on the ice." Looking down at my skates, he said, "I think if we tightened your laces that it would help."

He kneeled down and helped me tighten the laces on my skates. Johnny Miller was so kind and gentle while he tightened the strings on my skates. I think I started to fall in love with him right then.

⊶━━━━━━━━━⊷

For the next three years and three months, I saw Johnny ice-skating at the Beach City Dam or at the small-town festival in the summer. Since he played baseball for a town league in Wilmot, he liked pitching baseballs at the festival to knock over milk bottles for a prize. His brother Aden won a tall, stuffed clown for me once. Later on, when my senior classmates called me the class clown, I remembered that stuffed clown. My classmates probably never guessed how much I was trying to cover up the difficulties of my home life with my laughter and cheerful attitude.

From the time I was fourteen, summertime found me outside in the yard practicing twirling routines. I became a majorette at the beginning of eighth grade. Because I was in our yard so much, many of the Amish boys who had cars saw me while they were cruising around town, remembering me from ice-skating and festivals. Sometimes they stopped and chatted a while. I always enjoyed taking those little breaks and visiting with them.

One day a boy from Strasburg asked me if I wanted to ride around with him for a little while. I said, "Sure, why don't we go over to Wilmot and watch the ball game?" I didn't tell this boy that I was interested in going to Wilmot because I figured Johnny Miller would be playing ball there that day. I remembered him from the day we met at the ice-skating pond. This boy and I did go to Wilmot, and we watched the ball game for a while. Sure enough, Johnny was there. That's where my attention was: on him, not on the boy I was with. Johnny played ball as well as he ice-skated. Watching him play, I wished I could see him more often.

Suddenly, before the game was over, the boy I was with said, "Let's go. I've got to get home for my farm chores."

I thought, *Gee, a boy who helps his parents farm; he can't even be out on a date without having to leave to do chores. This boy is not for me!* I couldn't imagine that type of life for my future. During my grade-school years, sometimes boys from farms would come

Johnny in his baseball uniform in 1959.

to school with some interesting smells on them, and that's when I made up my mind that I was never going to marry a farmer.

That same evening, Johnny and his friend Milo Weaver were cruising around Beach City when they saw me and my friend Beverly walking across her lawn. Johnny pulled over his Harley and asked, "Would you like to go for a ride with me on my motorcycle? I saw you at the baseball game in Wilmot." Well, he didn't have to ask twice. I hopped on and away we flew, like down on a thistle.

We went out of town toward the dam where we ice-skated in the winter and rode around for about an hour. This wasn't the first time I had been on a motorcycle. I had ridden once or twice with my brother Garry on his motorcycle, but I really didn't know how to ride well. I was fantastically happy to be riding with Johnny, but when we came to a curve, Johnny leaned over with the bike into the curve. On instinct, I leaned the opposite direction, trying to keep us upright. Johnny's head popped around, and he said very firmly, "You can't lean in the opposite direction; you have to lean with me into the curve." From then on I always closed my eyes when we came to a curve, held tight to Johnny, and leaned with him as I felt him lean.

When he took me home Johnny asked me for a date the next Sunday evening, but I told him I had plans already. I sang with a group of seven girls called the Girls' Ensemble, and we were going to sing for baccalaureate services at the school that evening. He suggested he could pick me up after the services. I didn't want to tell him that I really wasn't allowed to date, because I really wanted to go on a date with him. So I told him to meet me at the schoolhouse after the service. I thought we would probably drive around the nearby town for a little while, just to be together, and then be home before my mom would miss me.

After baccalaureate, I stood on the curb, all keyed up with eager anticipation, waiting and wondering if he would really show up. My girlfriends waited with me and one of them asked, "Do you really think he is going to show up?"

I said, "I sure hope so!" And I did, because Johnny had intrigued me since that day he had bent over and tied the laces on my ice skates. There we stood, a little knot of girls fluttering around like a bunch of birds, talking and wondering, leaning over and looking toward the west.

"Look, here comes a blue car."

"It's him!"

Sure enough, along he came driving his brother's car. My friends waited right there, out of support—and curiosity—until I was in the car. "Bye, Marlene. Have fun."

We started toward the nearby town of Strasburg, but before we got there Johnny pulled in to an outdoor movie theater. I almost had a heart attack when we pulled in there. I knew I wasn't supposed to be dating, and I knew how long a movie might last.

When we stopped in the driveway to pay, I asked, "What do you think you are doing?"

He calmly answered, "Taking you to a movie."

I thought, *I should open the door and run back home. I'm not even supposed to be on a date, and here I am at an outdoor theater to watch a movie, which might take who-knows-how long.*

I knew it would look stupid if I bolted out of the car, so I tried to stay calm. But as soon as we hooked up the speaker, I emphatically told him, "We cannot do this!"

Of course, he looked at me, laughed, and asked, "Why not? You're sixteen."

I sat for a little while staring at the screen, anxious inside and not paying any attention at all to the movie, wondering how I was going to get myself out of this dilemma. Finally, I turned to Johnny. "I have to go home."

"The movie isn't nearly over," he said with his eyes still glued to the action in front of us.

I sat and stewed for a few minutes, then said louder and more insistently, "I have to go home or my mom will kill me!" After I repeated this two or three times, we finally left. By that time, I was really anxious about the reception I would get when I got home.

———

As we pulled up to my house, Mom was waiting at the door. Boy, was she angry. Right before I got out of the car, Johnny asked me if I would go to the ball game with him the next Sunday. I gulped and said yes, knowing that I had to do a lot of explaining to my mom—and a lot of begging—in order to see him again.

"Where have you been, and whose car have you been in?" Mom demanded.

I answered meekly, "Johnny Miller from around Alpine."

Mom was very upset that I wanted to date an Amish boy. Even though my parents had quite a few Amish friends, I guess having their daughter date an Amish boy was a little too much for them. She let me know in no uncertain terms what she thought of this whole proposition.

"You have plenty of school boys to choose from besides Amish boys," was her last shot. She didn't have much to say after that because I was sixteen—the age I had been told I would be allowed to date.

When she was done, she probably thought she'd had the last word and that would be the end of it. But I guess my independent spirit showed itself that day, because I thought, *I'm not going to listen. I will date. And I will date Johnny!*

That night when I went upstairs to bed, my mind was in turmoil, reflecting on what my mom had said: "Amish boys, no way . . . non-Amish boys, maybe."

I just couldn't put my finger on her dislike of the Amish. She really liked the Amish girl, Sara, whom she retained as a hired

girl. Thinking about this Amish question, I started reminisc-
ing about my contacts with the Amish and especially my buggy
rides with Sara's father, Sam Yoder. My parents knew him very
well, because my dad and mom and I went to his farm about
two and a half miles out of Beach City to train the beagle dogs
to run rabbits. When Sam came to town once or twice a month,
he tied up his horse and buggy to a hitching rail in a small
alcove across from our home. After much begging, I would get
to sit on his buggy. Soon that didn't seem to satisfy me, and I
asked if I could ride with him to the edge of town when he went
home after shopping.

I really enjoyed those Amish buggy rides with Sam, even
though the walk home was about a half mile, a fair distance for
a girl of eight. Sam always had a beaming smile and a tender
place in his heart for me.

Why did I love buggy rides? I mused now in my bed. *And how
can it be that Sam is Johnny's uncle?*

Coincidence? No. A thread in the tapestry of my life? Yes!

The next time Johnny came to pick me up, I just announced
I was going on a date. Mom looked up with shock, but didn't say
anything. And that's how I began officially dating.

Johnny was very polite when he came to pick me up. He
would come to the door, greet my dad with "Hello, Mr. Bailey,"
and quietly ask for me. If I wasn't ready, he would sit on a chair
and read the newspaper or watch the game on TV. Johnny
loved to read, and he always looked around for the newspaper
we subscribed to. He turned straight to the sports section to
catch up on his favorite teams' scores (he loved those Cleveland

Indians). Even if I was ready, many times he became so engrossed in reading the paper that I waited for him to finish.

Mom acted civil to Johnny. She never cussed or yelled at him, but when she turned the porch light on at the end of our dates, she swore at me if I didn't come right in. And she demanded in her recurrent theme, "What will the neighbors think?"

I loved that Johnny was well dressed, clean, and neat; his clothes were always in order. Being from a large family he couldn't afford expensive clothes, but he was very clean. He never made a fuss whatsoever, so I just couldn't see why Mom was not in favor of me dating him.

Johnny's parents were Old Order Amish and were very strict. At age twenty-one, Johnny was living at home and helping his dad farm, although he had not yet been baptized into the faith. There were six boys and four girls in his family. I didn't meet

Johnny at age four, holding his sister Susan's doll. Photograph taken at the farm on which he grew up.

most of Johnny's family while we were dating, because he knew they would not approve of him dating an "English" (non-Amish) girl or accept one into their family. I only knew about his family from what he told me. I did meet his two brothers who also played ball with him during the summer. These brothers later joined the Amish church and married Amish girls.

Johnny wanted to earn more than the twenty-five dollars in spending money he was getting every two weeks from his work on the farm. So after we had dated five months, he quit farming for his dad and went to work at the Ashery Cheese Factory at Fredericksburg to become a cheesemaker. He started making some big money—by *big money*, I mean $125 a month! He bought a 1956 Plymouth, which was a step up from using his motorcycle and his brother's car. I thought Johnny was really coming up in the world. Now, with a car, we wouldn't get caught in the rain, and it would surely be welcome during the coming winter.

4

Twirling, Singing, Cheerleading

I WAS A cheerleader in my seventh and eighth grades and a majorette during my seventh, eighth, ninth, and tenth grades at Beach City High. Although I planned to graduate from Beach City High School just like my brother Larry, who graduated in 1955, seven years before I did, a great disappointment came after my tenth grade. Beach City and the two little towns

Junior high cheerleaders (*from left*): Kay Stutz, Marlene, Trudy Haines, and Linda Fulton.

Majorettes for the marching band during the 1958 season (*from left*): Marlene, Linda Smith, Connie Gehring, Penny Wise, and Linda Brahler.

nearby consolidated their schools into one district. They called the consolidated school Fairless High School, but since it was in Navarre in the former Navarre High School building, we usually just called it Navarre. Now I had to ride the bus to and from my high school, which was now the largest in the district.

I hated that school. Riding the bus to school every day was very monotonous, and I was afraid I might throw up on the bus ride. I always got carsick as a little girl, and now I certainly didn't want to throw up on myself or ruin the seat. I had thrown up more than once riding the band bus. I got sick from the curves, opened the window, and let 'er fly. After I had done this a couple of times, the bus driver made me sit in the front and look out the window to keep from getting sick. Sometimes I sang with some of the other girls, and that helped, too.

Even with these difficulties, I still loved riding the band bus to games and events. It was exciting being with my friends and looking forward to our performances, but the ride to school every day wore on me.

I also didn't like the change of schools because they locked us in or out of the school for all kinds of reasons. We had never been locked in at Beach City High, but at Navarre that's exactly what they did to us. For a while, they locked us out of the school at lunch. Then when some boys got into trouble downtown during the noon hour, they locked us in the auditorium during lunch. Many times I asked myself how I would make it through those final two years of high school. Johnny kept convincing me to stay in school, however, and to continue in the band. He knew how much I enjoyed band and singing, and told me I would regret it if I dropped out. So I stayed.

I continued singing with my six friends in our Girls' Ensemble all through school. We loved to sing at various functions and had our favorite songs. We sang lots of different songs, including some songs we'd heard on the radio, like "Green Fields." We wrote down the words and then practiced learning the songs together. Some of the girls harmonized, but I

The Girls' Ensemble included (*front row, from left*): Ginny Bair, Kay Stutz, Marlene, Sherry Atkinson; (*back row, from left*): Ruthie Moody, Cheryl Wohlheter, and Linda Fulton.

Marlene's senior
photo, taken in 1962.

always sang the melody. Many of the songs we sang were about
faith, like "Amazing Grace" and "Bless This House."

The words in these songs about faith were very meaningful
to me and have come into my mind during many momentous
or difficult times. One of my favorites was "The Lord's Prayer."
Every time we sang that song, I got goosebumps. Singing with
these friends gave me joy each time we got together. During
study hall, we often practiced in the restroom. We also practiced and sang on the band bus, and we were asked to sing at
almost every school function. We never did get into bickering
or problems like most girls do in school. We just got along all
those years.

Mostly I got average grades all the way through school, but
once I was on the honor roll. Boy, I thought that was something.
But my biggest passion was being a majorette, so I worked even

harder during the summer before my senior year in hope of becoming the head majorette. For the first time in my life, I took special majorette lessons. Johnny was kind enough to take me to my lessons in Massillon each week. My mom never drove a car, and I wouldn't have even thought to ask my dad. Surely he wouldn't take me, because his whole life was wrapped up in his beagle dogs and field trials.

One week Johnny's car broke down as we were on our way to my lessons. We were coming to the outskirts of Massillon when his car started sputtering and jerking. Then it started to rain. Johnny pulled the car over and got out to look under the hood. When he couldn't figure out what was wrong with the car, he told me to start running, because we both knew the owner of Adelman's Dance Studio was a stickler for promptness. I had witnessed the mean looks and sometimes heard the chewing-out other girls received when they'd been late to their lessons. Since we were only four blocks away, I started running fast. I arrived, huffing and puffing and soaking wet, only five minutes late.

After taking lessons all summer, it was finally time for the yearly tryouts to be a majorette. Everyone who wanted to be a majorette had to do this each year. They also chose the head majorette at these auditions. I joined a group of hopeful girls gathered in the high school auditorium, waiting our turn to try out in front of each other. Time went on, girls went up and tried out, and I waited and waited for my name to be called. I was a nervous wreck and couldn't figure out why they didn't call me to perform. After about fifteen or twenty girls had tried out, they still hadn't called my name, so I reminded my band director that I was waiting. Instead of calling me to audition, the band director asked one of the judges to tell a story.

This judge was the woman from Adelman's Dance Studio, where I had taken lessons. I thought, *This is no time to tell a story.* Why in the world was she asked to tell a story now—in the middle of tryouts? But she proceeded to tell of my summer lessons with her: how I had worked so hard for months to improve my skills, how my boyfriend's car had broken down once and how I had run in the rain several blocks to try to get to my lesson on time. She told how I was panting like a dog when I got there—only five minutes late in spite of the rain and all the difficulties. She had decided that, since I had shown so much dedication and perseverance in working toward being

Marlene as head majorette for the Fairless High School Band. Photograph taken in 1961.

head majorette, she would give me that opportunity without me even needing to try out.

I almost fell over with amazement, and I think I cried. I just couldn't believe my ears. I really couldn't believe someone would care enough about me to allow me this opportunity without even auditioning. On top of that, I couldn't believe someone would say all the complimentary things she said about me. Knowing I had the respect and confidence of my twirling instructor and being given this honor of head majorette gave me a new determination. From then on, I tried harder to like school and to do my very best at everything.

Oh, how I worked hard to earn money for the things I needed for my school activities! I spent many hours and many days babysitting for fifty cents an hour. I even cleaned other people's houses in addition to the housework I did at home. That money bought my baton and boots and paid for all my lessons. But I didn't mind the work; I thought it was worth it all. I had wanted to be a majorette since I was a little girl taking dance lessons and watching that majorette on the TV show. After all those years of dreaming, I had finally made it.

The majorettes at Fairless High School; Marlene is second from left.

I did all our cleaning at home, cooked our meals, and washed the dishes while Mom went to work in the beer joint most nights. Mom washed the clothes, but she also watched soap operas and talked and talked on the telephone. It seemed to me that she was always talking on the phone, complaining about her health or her lack of money.

All the work and the activities I was involved with in school taught me lifelong skills. Working at home and for the extra things I needed taught me a work ethic. It also taught me to value money: how to save up for what I needed and how to be resourceful in earning. Being in the band, singing in the choir, and singing with the Girls' Ensemble in churches, for mother-daughter banquets, and for father-son banquets made me learn how to be prompt, how to use my time wisely, and how to be disciplined. I had no idea then how much this would help me later in life.

It made me cry when I heard my school in Beach City was being demolished. A school is a big part of what keeps a community together, especially in small towns. At first they left some of the smaller school buildings on the campus, but eventually they tore them down, too, and now there are no buildings remaining. I spent many, many happy, enjoyable hours at that school learning, going to dances, twirling, cheerleading, singing, and in band. Had I lived in the country, I'm sure I wouldn't have had those joyous opportunities that had shaped my life.

Finally June 2, 1962, arrived: the day for which I had waited for twelve years. I graduated from high school and got engaged the same night. I had long dreamed of getting married and having six children—three boys and three girls. It seemed my dream was beginning to come true.

5

Graduation, Engagement . . . and Anguish

JOHNNY PICKED ME up and took me to my graduation. I was hoping to get my ring that night, because we had already picked out our rings. One of my close friends had gotten engaged at Christmas, and I had been anxious for my turn since then. As we pulled up to the athletic field where graduation was to be held, Johnny turned to me, pulled a diamond ring out of his pocket, and put it on my finger. Was I ever happy! I practically flew out of the car.

Just then a woman named Lois came up, looked at my hand and asked, "Did you get engaged?" I proudly showed her my ring, and then all my girlfriends came to look.

After graduation, we went to Grandma Smith's for my graduation party, and all my favorite relatives were there. Grandma had the graduation party for me because Mom had never even given me a birthday party. I'm sure there was no way she would have thought to give me an even bigger graduation party. "Our house isn't nice enough," or "Our house isn't big enough," or "We don't have money to pay for the extra food," she would have said. So my loving Grandma Smith hosted my graduation party.

Marlene, age seventeen, and Johnny, age twenty-two, at her high school prom in 1961.

I was so happy, practically floating on clouds, when Mom put a big damper on the evening and on my mood. As I was walking from the living room back to the kitchen, Mom stopped me in the dining room and said, "Well, I heard you got engaged. Why didn't you tell me instead of Lois?"

I tried to explain to her that Lois had grabbed my hand, looking for a ring. Johnny and I had gone together for three years, so people were expecting that we would get married soon.

Mom was very angry and got mean. She couldn't understand why I wanted to marry Johnny. She taunted me with any petty thing she could think of against him: "His parents are Amish" and "He has a birthmark on his arm." She even said, "You'll probably have ugly children with birthmarks on their faces."

I couldn't believe Mom was saying these things to me, especially on this night. I felt like slapping her. Instead I just turned away, thinking, *Oh, she's trying to start something again.* This is what my brothers, my dad, and I often said. It seemed like every time there was something going on, she liked to make a big scene. Later in life I realized she was probably jealous because she'd never had a husband like Johnny. Johnny never hit me or swore at me. He was so kind, quiet, and gentle.

Although I was overjoyed at being engaged, that summer, fall, and winter were difficult for Johnny, and he could not agree to set a date for our wedding. Ever since we had started dating, Johnny had been thrown into a big conflict. He wanted to stay connected to his family, and deep in his heart he knew he eventually wanted to be Amish, but he also loved and wanted me.

In the heat of August I had a physical ordeal. During those days, Johnny and I made some mistakes and became physically intimate beyond what we should have. We loved each other very much. On a late Saturday afternoon when my parents were in Pennsylvania at a dog trial, Johnny came to inquire about my health. Because I was feeling so poorly, I was in my brother's bed downstairs. Johnny came directly in and sat on a chair near the bed. After we talked briefly, he put his head down and cried. The conflict in his soul was consuming him. Through tears he said, "I should walk out of your life forever, and never come back."

I took hold of his left hand, and begged him to be still. "Please never say or do anything like that, because I love you so much."

In the dead of winter I discovered I was pregnant. I begged again for us to get married, but Johnny kept putting it off. When I was about three months along, he bought a 10' x 50' trailer house in Massillon from my sister-in-law's sister. *Finally he's making a definite decision,* I thought. This made me feel we were at least making some progress toward getting married.

Our wedding was planned for April 14, 1963, at the Methodist church in Brewster. I knew my dad wouldn't pay for a big wedding, so I'd planned a bare-bones event. My dress was just what we called a "street dress." The only thing about it that resembled a wedding dress was that it was white. Since it was Easter time I knew there would be flowers at the church; otherwise I simply wouldn't have had any. I figured Dad couldn't afford to pay for a meal at the church, so there was no food ordered. He did say if anyone wanted to come to the restaurant in Strasburg, he might help pay for the meal. He never said if he would pay for sure, so Johnny felt that he had to have some extra money just in case he needed to cover this bill. I pitied Johnny so much because I knew this added expense really put him on the spot. He was doing all he could to scrape together enough money for our marriage, our honeymoon, and our life together, and here was another cost.

The night before the wedding we had a date, but Johnny just drove around aimlessly. He barely talked, and I could tell he wasn't happy. I just had a gut feeling something was going to happen, and it was not going to be something good.

This gut feeling is the reason that it didn't surprise me when, on our wedding day, he didn't show up at my house when it was time for us to go to the church. There I was, starting to zip the zipper on my dress, when the dreaded phone call came. I was afraid because of the talk that Johnny and I had had the night before, and I was worried that the wedding wouldn't take place.

After I hung up the phone, I went numb, my mind went blank, everything stopped, and I froze. Then, when my parents started yelling, the reality of my situation began to sink in. They barely got out the door when my brain said, *I've got to get to*

Johnny. Then another thought came even more clearly: *I have to get to Johnny's parents before my parents do.* With some determination, I quickly jumped into a skirt and sweater. I knew my mom and dad were going to be heading out to his family farm soon, and I wanted to be there first. I was hoping most of all to see Johnny, but I also doubted he would be there.

I talked my brother Franny into taking me. When we got to Johnny's parents' farm, I turned to Franny and said, "Just stay in the car." Although Franny was usually very independent, this was one time he seemed very willing to listen to me and stayed in the car.

I knocked, and Johnny's brother Paul opened the door. It seemed the family was ready and waiting for someone to come. They were assembled in the dining room, all lined up on a bench, all except Johnny. Right inside the door sat Johnny's brother Wayne; Wayne's wife, Lizzie; Johnny's mother, Saloma; his dad, Andy; and his sister Susan, who was very sick with diabetes. Their heads were down, and I could see they were very sad. I felt the sadness in the room. His brother Paul stood in the doorway of the room.

Try to imagine this little English girl bursting into their Amish home asking, "Where's Johnny?" and "Why won't he marry me?" Even though I was distraught, they were very calm and cordial. Nobody talked loudly or with disrespect. They didn't talk down to me like I was a little girl. I respected them for that, because I hadn't been taught that type of respect in my home.

They explained that Johnny was not there and invited me to have a seat, but I declined. I didn't want to stay, since Johnny wasn't there. I wanted to see Johnny. I needed to talk with him.

If I could just talk with him, maybe things would be all right. Maybe my world would go back into place.

Looking around, I began to feel sorry for them all. Johnny was their baby, and they felt he would leave the Amish for good if he married me. They also thought our marriage would probably end in divorce. They knew that Amish boys who marry English girls almost never come back to their Amish faith.

Until that morning, Johnny had not told his family that he was getting married and that I was pregnant. When he broke the news, the whole household cried and cried. Then the big question came: "Do you really want to marry this English girl or do you want to turn your life around and be Amish?" Johnny was in anguish, between a rock and a hard place. This was the same torment he had faced all these months and years while we were dating. His sense of responsibility toward me and toward our baby, his love for me and his love for his family, his desire possibly to become Amish someday: these were all the conflicting thoughts he had struggled with over and over in his mind. And all these had come into focus on this day.

His family had told him that nobody ever comes back to being Amish after marrying someone English, never mind the impossibility of an English girl turning Amish. Looking at the pain on the faces of his loved ones, he had chosen to be Amish over marrying me.

<hr>

This was the scene that was fresh in the minds of his family. As I stood there, Johnny's brother Wayne began to speak. It was obvious he had been the one chosen to speak, because everyone else sat there silently.

With tears in his eyes and compassion in his voice, he said, "Whatever the cost, we are willing to pay—all your medical expenses and all the birthing expenses. Lizzie and I have talked it over, and we are willing to take the baby to raise."

I came up short at that. I didn't have to think very long before I said, "No. Thanks, but no thanks. This baby belongs to Johnny and me, and I will never give it up."

"Okay, that is your decision to make," Wayne said. "But we are still willing to help you with the expenses."

"No," I said. "I don't know how this baby will be paid for. However, nobody else is going to pay for it. It's Johnny's. Why should someone else have to pay for it?"

After a little more conversation, I said, "I'd better go. But I want you to tell Johnny that he *cannot* call me on the phone and tell me he won't marry me. He *must* come to me and tell me that he doesn't love me."

I can't imagine what they thought when they heard me say this, but I was determined to have Johnny look me in the face and tell me he didn't love me and wouldn't marry me. Even though this was a difficult conversation, they continued to be respectful to me, and I was respectful to them. They told me that they would tell him what I had said.

I turned to go, my hand on the door, anxious to leave before my parents showed up. His brother Paul said, "You certainly had a hex on Johnny."

In the same tone I threw back, "Did *I* drive his car to my house, or did *he*?"

My brother and I drove out. As we neared the end of their lane, here came Mom and Dad. She started screaming at me from their car because I hadn't stayed at home as she had ordered. Franny and I drove back home, my heart as heavy as it had ever been. The pain was sharp and physical, and the anguish lay so heavy on me I could hardly move.

When we got home, I went straight to bed. I didn't sleep all night. I just cried and cried and cried, and for the first time I really prayed to the Lord. Oh, yes, I had prayed when I had gone to church, but this was totally different. Now I was in dead earnest. Sometimes it takes heartbreaking circumstances like this to make us truly communicate with God. Over and over the events of the day played out in my mind. I pleaded with God, "If you'll give Johnny to me as my husband, I'll do anything for you." Later when I completely surrendered my life to Jesus Christ, I remembered that prayer and began to understand it.

The next day, Monday, I went to the Ashery Cheese Factory to see Johnny. Since we hadn't gone on our honeymoon, I assumed he would probably be at work. I asked Grandpa Bailey if I could use his car, but he said no. He didn't want me to go see Johnny because he was so angry with him leaving me practically standing at the altar. After I begged for the car, he finally gave in and let me take it because I was so desperate to see Johnny.

It was late afternoon when I arrived at the Ashery. I had timed it to arrive before Johnny would be off work, but late enough that he would be nearly finished. I walked into the big cheese-making room where Johnny was working on four big, two-hundred-pound wheels of Swiss cheese. He totally ignored me. He didn't look up, didn't look at me, and just kept working.

So I went and stood by the doorway of the boiler room, where I watched and waited for an opportunity to talk with

Johnny working at the Ashery Cheese Factory in 1964.

him. His boss was there at first, and when he left, his boss said, "Hi, Marlene," as he went by me and walked right up the stairs to his home in the story above. Johnny's boss must have known some of what had taken place the day before, since Johnny came back to work and didn't go on a honeymoon. After his boss left, Johnny began cleaning up, scrubbing, and sweeping to wrap up his workday.

I waited for about an hour until Johnny came over to where I was standing, and, without looking up, went into the boiler room. I followed him.

"Tell me to my face that you don't love me or want me," I said.

But he wouldn't or couldn't say that. He just looked at the floor, and during that entire time we were in there, he never looked at me once.

Desperately I told him, "I'll let you do anything you want to do if only you will marry me." I was such a nervous wreck from all the trauma of the day before and from being awake the entire night. All my senses were on edge. All night I had lain awake praying, crying, and desperately seeking answers for what I could do.

Finally Johnny started talking. The main thing he talked about was how angry and mean my mom was when she talked to his parents.

"What did Dad have to say?" I asked, thinking he probably had quite a lot to say also.

"Your dad was very civil about it all," Johnny said. "But your mom said she hoped my parents go to h— because they talked me out of marrying you. She also said that she and your dad were going to call the law to turn me in for taking you with me to some local taverns and for getting you pregnant." She had said this because I was only nineteen instead of twenty-one, which was legal age. It seemed to me that she was throwing anything she could in their faces to make them pay for the wrong done to me and my family.

This threat really concerned Johnny's parents, because they didn't want him going to jail. They had already experienced that with his brother Paul. After filing as a conscientious objector to avoid being drafted into the military, Paul had done alternative service at a Cleveland hospital. He had filed as a conscientious objector because military service was against his nonresistant Amish faith. Also, for religious reasons, Paul would not work on Sundays at the hospital. He was sent home for refusing to work on Sundays, and eventually he was arrested. He spent a short time in jail.

When Mom said "jail," it made Johnny's parents back off their firm stand. Johnny was the baby of the family, and they did not want to face having him go to jail. They began to think it might be wise for Johnny to come and talk with me at least.

That evening at the supper table, Mom said, "Well, what happened?"

"He's coming tomorrow night to talk to us."

"Johnny probably thinks the baby isn't his and that's why he didn't marry you," she threw back.

I answered, "God knows whose baby it is and that's all that matters." My answer surprised even me. When did I ever talk about God? Maybe it surprised my mom, too, because there was very little said at that dinner table after that.

Johnny came on Tuesday evening and talked to my mom and me. He was very solemn when he came in, offering no smile of greeting. He sat down at the kitchen table and in a gruff tone said, "I'll marry her, and we'll do it on Saturday."

I felt like a bystander listening to them. No one was talking to me. They were just talking about me and deciding my life. He was still very angry about what my mom had said to his parents. After a little more talk, Mom almost ruined everything when she said, "If you don't want her after you're married for a while, you can divorce her."

I almost fell off my chair.

At this, Johnny got up from his kitchen chair and walked right out the front door. I went running after him. He got into his car and started driving. I grabbed the door on the passenger side and jumped in while the car was still moving. He drove around and around in silence. Finally he pulled into a side street, parked, and turned to me. "Do you feel just like your mother about marriage and divorce?" he asked.

"No," I said truthfully. "If difficulties arise, I really believe people can work at a marriage and not divorce. I really want to be married for life." That was the end of our conversation.

After that he took me home and said, "We'll get married on Saturday at the church with only Yost Weaver as our best man and his girlfriend, Clara, as your maid of honor. No other people can be there except the preacher's wife."

So much for all my plans for a nice wedding day, all those dreams a girl has her whole life of a glorious wedding—a beautiful dress, lots of flowers, and being surrounded by happy people. In my mind, those dreams just tumbled down like a crumbling building and lay in a heap. But I knew I loved Johnny and he loved me, and that was the most important thing.

On April 20, 1963, Johnny and I said our marriage vows at the church with two friends, the preacher, and his wife present. I wore the dress I had bought for my wedding. I also wore a beautiful cream-colored coat with a fur collar and big, bold buttons Grandma Smith bought me. She said she wanted me to have something nice for my wedding, and the weather was still cool enough for a coat.

Most of the people who had come for our wedding the Sunday before never gave us the gifts they had brought. Only my parents, my grandparents, and my beloved aunts gave us wedding gifts. Grandma Bailey gave us a six-piece set of utensils and a copper-bottom saucepan with handles that were riveted on. I used that pan for more than forty-seven years for popping popcorn. What a pan to hold up under all those hard years of use. Grandma Smith gave us a beautiful set of china

Marlene and Johnny on their wedding day, April 20, 1963.

with about six place settings, which she had bought at a sale. I boldly asked Dad for the set of stainless steel cookware he had bought at a sale a couple of years earlier and had stored away in a closet. My poor mom—I don't know why she didn't say, "I'm going to use those right away," and take them for herself. Maybe God had them planned for me. I guess the rest of our family and friends thought our marriage would never last anyway, so why bother with gifts?

As of now, it has lasted fifty-two years. Amen, Lord!

6

Wonders of the World

WE WENT TO Mid's tavern in Wilmot for our wedding supper and had spaghetti and meatballs and a salad. That was the first time I had ever eaten lettuce salad. I liked it, and I really liked the French dressing, too. Mom had never made salad for us. The only time we had seen lettuce was when Mom was dieting and it would appear on her plate. But she had never offered any to us.

After supper, Johnny and I returned to our home, our little trailer in the Perry Heights area of Massillon, Ohio. I really loved that little trailer, as it was our very own home. We were both elated that night, glad the ordeal of the last six days was over. We didn't even mention those days.

We awoke with smiles on our faces at five o'clock the next morning, the usual time Johnny went to work. We were so happy finally to be together and to go on our delayed honeymoon. Our suitcases were packed in our 1960 Oldsmobile convertible, and we were very excited to go out of state for the first time as we aimed for Niagara Falls, both the New York and Canadian sides.

We started out going the speed limit of seventy miles per hour on I-90, but after two hours of people passing us, including

The trailer that Marlene and Johnny lived in after they were married.

state patrol cars, we put the hammer down at around ninety. We laughed and laughed as we raced along and commented to each other, "The cops on this interstate don't seem to care how fast we go!"

We stopped a few times at rest areas to stretch our legs and had lunch at a small restaurant off the beaten path. I can't remember what I had for lunch. I was just so elated to be going on my first vacation, my honeymoon, and especially that I had Johnny at my side. We stopped at a little motel not far from the falls, close to the Niagara River. We could even hear the sound of the falls from there. We were so giddy and excited; it was like a dream! After paying the motel fees we took our suitcases to our room, showered, and then headed straight for the falls.

The majesty and power before us were overwhelming. The thunderous roar is continuous and so moving. We had never experienced anything like this before. Johnny said, "To think it flows and flows for thousands of years and never stops." And still it just goes on and on.

Marlene at Niagara Falls, April 1963.

Many a daredevil has gone over the Canadian Horseshoe Falls; because there are so many boulders and rocks on the American side, it would be certain death to attempt going over there. We went down an elevator to get a closer look and feel the mist. I struggle to describe something so awesome. The feeling of sheer power and endless energy created a feeling inside us that just went beyond words.

The next day we went to the Horseshoe Falls on the Canadian side. We thought things couldn't get any better after our experience with the American Falls the first evening, but we were mistaken. The mist and the freshness of the air was overpowering as we stood by a railing that was almost on the edge of the falls. The roar was so loud I had to yell for Johnny to be able to hear me: "If this rail wasn't here, the pull from the water would be so great I'd topple in."

Next we went to the Whirlpool, where a cable car that could hold about ten people traveled on a rail high above. Johnny

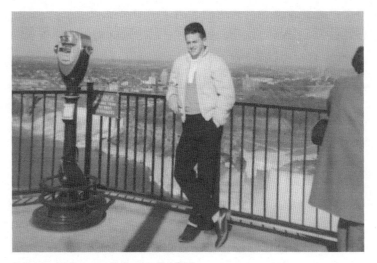

Johnny at Niagara Falls, April 1963.

begged me to go on it, and I begged him not to. He partly won, because he rode on it by himself. I whimpered before he stepped on, "I finally have you as a husband, and now you want to go on this dangerous ride. The cables will probably break, and you'll be gone forever." He just smiled, laughed, and gave me a reassuring hug. Then he pulled away and was gone.

I held my breath for what seemed like forever. When he was halfway over I saw his arm raised. I wondered what he was doing, because it didn't look like he was waving to me. When he came back he said, "I threw a penny one direction, but it flew completely the other way. The force of the wind from the falls made it go the wrong way." He had followed it with his eyes. He could only afford to toss a penny because we were on such a tight budget.

After spending all day at the falls, we still weren't satisfied. The majesty and power drew us back as if we were mesmerized. We went to a quaint restaurant for supper, then showered to freshen up and returned to the Canadian side. We wanted to see the colored lights at night on Horseshoe Falls. We both commented, "This is beautiful, what man does with lights and what God does with his hands."

We also went up the Skylon Tower on the Canadian side. It was so tall that my knees were shaking just looking at it. I'm terribly afraid of heights, but Johnny talked me into taking the tower ride up in the elevator. He said, "Please, please go; you'll really like it once you're on the top." He was right; I did like it. But I didn't love it. I was still reeling from the elevator ride. I had always hated elevators; they gave me head rushes and a feeling of dread. I had the irrational fear during the ride that it would never stop. At the end of the ride, I said, "Thank goodness the elevator stopped or else we would have shot out into the clouds."

The deck on top was surrounded by high railings with coin-operated telescopes. We loved looking through the telescopes because we could see for miles, and we could also see the falls close up. Looking through the lenses, we felt again the rush of the water and the powerful force it created. We were too shy to ask anyone to take our picture together, so we only took pictures of each other standing at the rail.

After seeing and experiencing one of the Seven Wonders of the World, we traveled east all day to Utica, New York. Johnny had traveled much in his imagination through reading books, and he wanted to experience some of the places he had read about, so he wanted to go to the Adirondack Mountains and forest preserves. We stayed in a motel in Utica that night.

After breakfast the next morning there was a slight rain as we traveled into the mountains and along many lakes, but before long it started to snow. It snowed buckets and buckets, and we realized we were in a regular blizzard. I was so afraid that I didn't say one word, which is highly unusual for me. Johnny was quiet while he was driving, trying to see and drive in this blinding snowstorm. Tension sat between us like a physical presence as we rode along, mile after mile, in silence. I was sure we were going to get stranded and die in the snowstorm.

Out of nowhere, we came upon a snowplow lumbering along in front of us. Thankful to have this guiding pilot, we followed it most of the way back to Utica. As we drove, the snow eventually turned to rain and we arrived safely back at our hotel. We were relieved as we went to our room, thankful we had come back alive.

The next day we were on the road again to Pittsburgh, Pennsylvania, to the Pittsburgh International Airport. Johnny loved to travel and was fascinated with airplanes, so he had planned this stop as another first experience for both of us. At that time, people could walk onto an outside deck and look down on the planes to watch the loading and unloading, the takeoffs and landings. I just could not believe how loudly the engines roared. A feeling of joy and wonder rose in me as I experienced the power in these large machines. I was so thankful to Johnny for bringing me here. I had never seen a plane up close before.

After a week of seeing sights we had only read about or dreamed of, we were back in our little mansion in Massillon, back in the real world. Johnny had to be at work at the cheese factory bright and early Monday morning.

For years we relived those magical days of our honeymoon together. Many times we told our children we wanted to go back there again, but it would definitely have to be in summer. No braving spring snowstorms again for us.

Two months later we moved our trailer from Massillon to the grounds of the Ashery Cheese Factory. Johnny's boss wanted us to move there so we could take care of the occasional after-hours customer and save money on gas. We had lived over twenty-five miles away, and it cost a lot in gas every day for Johnny to go back and forth. Because we were willing to wait on the after-hours customers, we didn't have to pay rent for our lot.

This was my first experience living in the country, and I really loved it. I loved the peace and quiet and how dark it was at night. In the country there's just more freedom; there isn't always someone looking over your shoulder, as is often the case in town. Then, too, the people who lived around us treated us with respect. I liked that. I was no longer treated as a child but as a married woman.

I had always loved animals, and being in the country gave me lots of opportunities to watch people with their horses. Even the hogs were interesting to me. When Johnny went out to dump slop—the whey and scraps from the cheese process—in the neighbor's hog pen, I went with him. The hogs came running and squealing and rooting the trough. I said, "My goodness, they are eating like hogs!"

"They *are* hogs," Johnny said, with a little grin.

"Oh yeah. You're right," I said, and felt like a silly city girl.

Ever since watching Roy Rogers and Dale Evans and riding my cousin Davy's horse, I had wanted a horse, and I loved watching the Amish men come with their horses and carts to fill their milk cans. I was very curious and asked many questions. Right across the road was a blacksmith shop, and I often thought, *I need to go over and watch him.* I'm sure I just about drove him crazy with all the questions I asked. "How many nails do you have to put into that shoe?" "Doesn't that hurt the horse's foot?" I didn't even know enough to call it a hoof! Years later I ran into this blacksmith and he laughed when he saw me. He said, "You were such a nice girl and so interested in my work." Maybe he hadn't minded my curiosity and questions so much after all.

Two months after moving to the Ashery, we had Michael Jay, on August 19, which happened to be my brother Franny's birthday. Michael was born at 11:45 p.m. at Wooster Hospital. When the nurse placed him in Johnny's arms and left the room, Johnny announced to me, "I want you to know, whether you like it or not, he's going to learn to speak German." Pennsylvania German, also called Pennsylvania Dutch, is the first language of most Amish people, and Johnny wanted our children to be able

Johnny and Marlene holding Michael when he was a few weeks old.

to speak it. I had no problem with this at all. From that day on, Johnny never talked any English to him.

It was awesome to see how perfect Michael was. To think how God creates a baby! I couldn't quit looking at him.

All the babysitting I had done for other people's children had not prepared me, however, for Michael's nonstop crying. He cried almost 24/7 for three months. After a few weeks of this, I was so drained and frustrated that I was about ready to pack him up and ship him anywhere else so I could have some peace. Finally, relief came when we discovered he fell asleep when I swept the carpets with the vacuum or when we took him for a ride in the car. We'd no sooner start up State Road 241 toward Mount Eaton to visit our friend Yost Weaver than Michael would fall asleep. Even when he was older, Michael loved to hear a motor running. What a relief! I felt the stress drain out of me just like water draining out of a bathtub when Michael finally slept and gave me some peace.

The other nine children I would have after Michael were such contented babies. It made me wonder whether Michael's discontent as a baby had something to do with all the crying I did before he was born.

7

Kitchen Sink Conversion

AFTER MICHAEL WAS born I was home by myself a lot, while Johnny was either working or playing baseball. I started to be very jealous and possessive, and I took to swearing more. I was miserable, and I was making Johnny miserable. I didn't like myself at all. God was convicting me of my need for him, but I didn't realize it at the time.

Johnny never gave me any reason to be jealous, but I had many long hours alone and my mind began to go places it shouldn't. With the baby's incessant crying and being alone so much, I dreamed up scenarios in which Johnny would leave the ball game and go to a bar or meet another woman. I even thought that maybe he didn't want to be with us because he had this crying baby at home. In my loneliness and frustration, I worked myself up into believing some of these fantasies. Then when Johnny would come home I would yell at him, accusing him of the things I had imagined.

True to his character, Johnny would calmly and plainly say, "I wasn't doing anything." The devil was playing havoc with my mind. I didn't know then that if we don't rein in our thoughts, they can really go to the wrong places. I was learning some hard lessons.

Michael and I weren't allowed to go visit Johnny's parents, since we weren't Amish. Even though I had grown up around the Amish and had married Johnny, I didn't understand much of the Amish culture. I took this separation as a personal rejection, and I could just imagine what they might have against me. Day after day, as I mused over these feelings, they grew and grew until I became convinced that his parents hated me. It wasn't until much later that I found out this wasn't so at all. I also later came to believe that Satan has a way of putting such thoughts in our minds and twisting our thinking, always for his destructive purposes.

In the short time after our marriage, I was becoming an angry, jealous, distrustful person—someone I never thought I would be. I hated my accusations and spiteful attitude, but each time one of these episodes happened I seemed powerless to control myself or my emotions.

Johnny loved and missed his parents very much, so he visited them every two or three weeks. When he came home from a visit he always brought eggs, meat, and canned goods. Johnny noticed I didn't eat any of the food sent from his parents, and asked me why. I told him I figured the food was just for him.

Then it all came tumbling out. "Your parents must hate me because of the circumstances of our marriage and because of all the problems with my mom during that time," I blurted. Johnny assured me that his parents loved me and wanted me to enjoy the food, too. So we began sharing the delicious food from his family.

Every time Johnny came home from visiting his family he was low in spirit. He sat around in a quiet way, seeming to be in a pensive, reflective mood, and I heard him crying in the night. He missed them and their way of life so much that it caused him great pain. Hearing Johnny's grief hurt my heart, and I grieved for his loss. Apparently it was hard on his parents, too, because one of his family members hinted once that maybe it would be better if he didn't come back and visit.

But at the end of each visit, his mom always said before he left, "I'm praying for you all. Please come and visit us again."

Johnny had to get up so very early every day to haul in the milk for making cheese, so Sunday mornings were often our only time to talk together, as we had the morning to lie in bed a little later. One Sunday we slept in until about ten o'clock. After we woke up, we were just lying in bed and got to talking about Johnny's family, and about how they were praying for us.

"Us?" I puzzled. "Why would they be praying for me?" Again, I felt I had been such a bad girl that they surely hated me.

"Oh, no," Johnny said. "My mom and dad would never hate anybody." In all the years we had dated, Johnny had only had good things to say about his parents. He *never* said anything derogatory.

I thought, *Wouldn't it be nice to have parents like that?* I could surely find many, many faults with my parents. And it was even more amazing to me that his parents would not only *not* hate me but actually be praying for me.

When the novelty of that thought wore off, another thought came: *What would they* specifically *be praying for?* So I asked Johnny.

"Well, they thought . . ." Johnny began. "They thought maybe you would want to be Amish."

I was astounded. That thought had never entered my head. The first summer after we were married, I sometimes went with Johnny on his Saturday evening route to pick up milk from some of the Amish. I often saw some Amish kids come running out, and some of them were very dirty. I said, "I could never have my kids looking like that."

"No," Johnny said. "Being Amish doesn't mean being dirty. Cleanliness is just the same with the Amish as with the English. It's a matter of personal grooming."

The few glimpses I had into the Amish community left me with the impression that the women all wore very long dresses, black high-top shoes, and very large *Kapps*, and had children who weren't kept very clean.

"Oh, no," Johnny said. "My mom wears regular shoes, and not all the Amish wear those very long dresses and large caps."

After we had explored this interesting and novel subject for a while, Johnny said that his sister Susan was also praying for me. Susan was diabetic and still lived at home. Later I would learn that her prayers definitely made a difference in our lives.

When Michael was about one and a half months old, Johnny's brother Aden came to visit. We had a very long talk about how long eternity is. Aden described it to me this way: "If one seagull carried one grain of sand at a time from all the beaches in the world until he had emptied them, that would be just the beginning of eternity."

That thought kept going around and around in my head for some time. Thinking about eternity and how long it was made me wonder: *Where am I going to end up during that long span of time?* Another thought also constantly repeated itself for days in my head: "The fear of the Lord is the beginning of wisdom" (Psalm 111:10).

I started listening to Christian radio, and my sin began weighing very heavily on my mind. When we were dating, Johnny and I had sometimes listened to a popular Christian radio speaker while sitting out in his car in front of our house. Many times those sermons sparked deep conversations about God between us. I heard their preaching and thought, *Wow. I don't hear things like this at church.* I loved listening to music on the radio, and then sometimes a preacher would come on, or some Christian music. So it was familiar to me, and even pleasant, to tune the radio to some of these Christian programs to listen and think.

One evening toward the latter part of October, while Johnny was working at the cheese house, I was washing dinner dishes. While I was working, I started earnestly asking God a question. This was the question that had been troubling me since I had that talk about eternity with Aden. I asked God, "Where will I go when I die?"

I heard the answer in my heart as plainly as if God had spoken out loud.

"Hell."

My shoulders bowed as if a heavy weight like a load of bricks had come over me.

"No!" I cried out. Surely I wouldn't be going there.

Maybe I hadn't heard correctly, so again I asked, "Where will I go when I die?"

Again I heard the answer plainly: "Hell."

"No, no, no. I *never, never, never* want to go there!" The anguish was unbearable.

"God," I pleaded from deep down in my pain, "please just tell me where will I go when I die?"

"Hell." The answer came for the third time, and the weight and reality almost crushed me.

I started crying and just couldn't stop. Tears streamed down my cheeks, mingling with the sudsy water. I felt the heaviness of my life and all the things I had done wrong pressing on me until I was physically bowed over.

Then and there, right in the kitchen of our little trailer home, I asked God to come into my heart. "God, I totally, totally want to give my life to you," I prayed. "Take this hurt and all these evil things out of me. Forgive me for all the wicked things I have done. I can't keep living like this, so you have to take over my life. I want to turn my life around, and you have to do it. I just want to live for you from now on."

My prayer was answered, and immediately I felt such incredible joy! The heavy load of my sin flew off me. I took some deep breaths and tried to focus. I looked down, fully expecting to see huge bricks lying on the floor at my feet, because I knew I was no longer carrying that load of guilt and sin.

Just imagine me, a young mother, standing at the kitchen sink in our little trailer and fully realizing for the first time what a wonderful God we have. The tears continued to flow, but now they were tears of joy. My heart started singing "How Great Thou Art" and "Amazing Grace." Unbelievable peace flooded into me, and I couldn't stop smiling and laughing. Incredible joy coursed through me as the old words of the hymn now had deep personal meaning: how he saved a wretch like me, how I once was lost but now am found, how I was blind, but now I see.

I ran out of the trailer to the cheese factory to tell Johnny what had happened. Although my feet were pumping hard, I felt so light that it seemed like I was floating across the little bridge Johnny had made for us to cross the creek. I flew into the cheese house and searched around until I found Johnny in the warm cellar, where the big wheels of cheese were processing.

The words tumbled out of my mouth: "God has forgiven me . . . I'm going to heaven . . . I was standing at the kitchen sink and . . ." Johnny just stood there looking at me, stunned. He could hardly believe me. This type of sudden, emotional conversion was not the normal process for the Amish. They are very orderly and reserved. They make a decision to join the church, they take classes of instruction, and then they are baptized.

Here I was bubbling over with happiness, peace, and joy, and it was unbelievable to him. Then I told him the words that would change our lives: "I think I want to be Amish."

That was even more unbelievable to him. I was actually jumping up and down for joy, I was so happy. I asked, "When can we go to your family home?"

Johnny was speechless. He just looked at me, trying to process what I was saying and doing. Finally he answered in his steady way, "Well, we'll wait a couple of days and see if you still feel the same."

We waited for those few days, and I knew I was different and Johnny knew it too. First, we noticed I wasn't swearing anymore. My jealousy and anger had disappeared, too. What a miracle a prayer can bring! My whole life was changed in an instant. Johnny never asked me to be Amish, but the conviction came to me with my conversion to Christ.

I'm not saying that when a person is converted to Christ he or she has to become Amish. Not at all. But for me, it was the natural choice. It gave me peace and contentment to adopt this lifestyle and to love my husband enough to make him happy, which made me happy in the Lord.

Over time, Johnny came to realize that the change in my life was permanent and that my desire to be Amish had not diminished. From that day in the kitchen, the Bible had new meaning for me as I read the Holy Word. It became personal and relevant to me and my life. I started as a babe when Christ came into my heart, knowing little about the Christian life. But over the years, as I have read the Bible and learned from others, I have grown in my Christian faith. As we know, we are supposed to grow in the faith. That is exactly what the Lord has done for Johnny and me all through these years.

Part II

8

Getting Dressed in Amish Ways

IT WASN'T PEACHES and cream or high mountains after my conversion. Oh, no. We went through many valleys. First, we really had to think, plan, and pray about what to do next after I had made the decision to turn Amish. Remember, Johnny never asked me to be Amish; he only told me his family was praying for us. To become Amish, we would have to live close to his parents' home and home church. Since there was no place for sale in that district for about two years, we stayed put but began to make our plans for the big change.

One of our first decisions in those early preparation days was to buy a pickup. This must have puzzled some of Johnny's relatives. I'm sure they wondered why we bought another vehicle, besides the car we already had, if we were working toward being Amish. But we decided we had to do something to make more money. Not only did we have a new baby, but we also had car and trailer payments. Johnny only made $175 a month at the cheese factory, and we were barely scraping by. We did have a bonus by being provided with all the milk, cheese, and cream we wanted from the factory. That extra food surely kept us alive through many tight times.

Johnny made racks for the sides of our pickup and put a tarp over the top so he could use it for all kinds of purposes. Besides hauling animals, he also transported Amish people to and from sales. The women sat in front with him and the men rode in the back. So from the time of our early marriage, Johnny worked two or more jobs.

Johnny's boss owned a little piece of land across from the cheese factory. He told Johnny that we could use this land to raise some pigs if we were interested. We could feed them with the whey and other scraps from the cheese process until they were ready for market. So Johnny started his third job. He played baseball two nights and one day a week, and made cheese six days a week and on Saturday nights. In the summer he also transported Amish to sales and doctor visits. Oh, and he raised pigs. I'll tell you one thing: you can take the boy off the farm, but you can't take the farm out of the boy!

Johnny worked very hard at his jobs, and he worked hard figuring out ways to support us. Even with all his hard work and ingenuity, things were often tight financially. There were times in our marriage when we didn't have two dimes to rub together. But we had love for our Savior and for each other, and that love kept us going.

Most of the Amish around the Ashery belonged to a slightly different sect from the one Johnny's parents belonged to, but they were almost all very accepting of our son Michael and me. The women wore dresses clear to their ankles and usually high-top shoes. The Amish men wore longer hair and the brims on their hats were very wide.

Having grown up in town, I was used to having people around me, so I often visited my close neighbors. The two places I went most were Blacksmith Aden Troyer's and Jonas L. Miller's. Jonas's wife, Fannie, helped me in many ways to understand why the Amish women do things the way they do. She canned a lot and had a beautiful garden. During my visits I often asked Fanny questions about her Amish faith and way of life. She was very patient with me and answered my questions, always backing up her answers with Scripture.

Out of all the people we knew at the Ashery and our little community there, we told only two people that we were going to turn Amish in the future. We didn't want everyone to know because we thought they would not understand why we didn't just do it right away. But I knew, and Johnny did too, that this was going to be a life-changing move for us. I felt I had to learn to sew better and understand more of the Amish ways. We still did not know where we could live.

It's easy to turn from Amish to English, as far as how to live. One thing that's easy is that you can buy all your clothes instead of making them. It's easier to jump into a vehicle and drive than to learn to harness a horse and get it into a buggy.

But to go from English to Amish? Now that's a different story.

In November 1963, the time was approaching for us to go to Johnny's family home for the first time together. Since we had made the decision to be Amish, Johnny's parents had invited us to spend Thanksgiving Day at their home.

Johnny's sister-in-law Lizzie had taken me under her wing to help me get ready for this visit and learn Amish ways. She only had one child, a son named Johnny, and she seemed the obvious person to help me because of her small family. Lizzie said she would gladly and very willingly help me sew my first Amish dress. She offered to make the covering, or *Kapp*, for me. I knew just from looking at these *Kapps* that they were too detailed for my sewing skills.

Lizzie bought some green cotton material—green was her favorite color. I drove our car over to her place, and the fun began. We used her treadle sewing machine, which was familiar to me. I had taken homemaking in school and had used a treadle machine there. We had a few electric and some treadle machines in class, but most of the girls made a dash for the electric sewing machines while I was content to finish my projects on the non-electric treadle. So the rhythmic rocking motion of my feet on the treadle was not new to me.

I had made dresses and blouses for myself, but making an Amish dress was different. Putting a zipper in a garment had been the hardest part, so I liked the fact that Amish dresses didn't have zippers. It took me two days to get that dress completed, and I was a little embarrassed that it took so long. A week or so later, Lizzie sent the covering back with Johnny when he was there visiting.

Thanksgiving Day arrived, and with it came the time for me to put on my Amish dress and covering for our visit to Johnny's family home. I was excited to put them on because I was excited to get to be with Johnny's family. I found out right away that wearing an Amish dress was a little different and tricky for me. Because there is no zipper, the women just use straight pins up the front and on the waist to keep it closed. Well, I had a problem with using straight pins, because I was afraid of getting poked. I gingerly threaded those pins in as carefully as I could, but each time I felt a little prick, it reminded me of getting shots at the doctor's. I had never liked needles. When I did have to get a shot, I just couldn't stand to watch. My hands would sweat, and I looked the other way in anticipation of the needle stick. Throughout the day I kept getting poked by those little pins, and it made me so uncomfortable. Later on, as I learned a little Pennsylvania German, I would say *gicks*. Those pins would *gicks* me. Even to this day, I still have problems with straight pins in my clothes!

Then came time for the covering. I put my hair up, which wasn't unusual. I often wore my hair up because I couldn't stand hair hanging in my eyes. But putting the *Kapp* over it surely was different. I thought I looked funny, with this white, stiff *Kapp* perched on my head. And how was I supposed to keep it on? It wanted to fall off right away, so I thought I'd put a bobby pin on each side. At least that worked!

It stayed on, and away we went for our visit.

When I arrived, I saw that the women were using straight pins to hold their *Kapps* on their heads. I wondered how they could stand to put straight pins in their heads. That surely must hurt. I was having enough trouble with the pins in my dress poking me here and there all day.

In spite of the newness of the dress and the *Kapp* and the prickly annoyance of the pins, I loved that Thanksgiving Day. First came the warm welcome I received from each member of the family. As I looked into their eyes, I sensed the love and peace that I had been looking for; the acceptance and close family ties drew me in. Right off, I felt that here was a place

I could belong. I enjoyed the entire day immensely. When we sat down to the Thanksgiving meal, I was overwhelmed by the amount and variety of the food. That large Amish table was burdened with overflowing dishes of fried chicken, mashed potatoes, gravy, dressing, several salads, fruit, and Amish date pudding—Johnny's favorite.

Looking at my plate, Johnny's sister-in-law asked, "Aren't you having any dressing?"

"No, I don't care for dressing. My mom's dressing is terrible. She makes it with raw oysters, bread, milk, eggs, and spices, and stuffs it in the turkey."

"Well, this is Amish dressing. Maybe you should try a little; it's really quite good and not at all like the English dressing." I gingerly sampled it and discovered that they were right. This dressing was *soooo* good that I had seconds. With that first bite of Amish dressing, I began a big downfall into my love of eating. That dressing was rich, buttery, and delicious—and also fattening. From then on I haven't been able to resist Amish dressing—I love eating it and making it.

I had brought a dish to share for the meal—Jell-O with whipped cream, pineapple, and miniature marshmallows. Johnny's family was very surprised that my dish looked good and was tasty. They had never whipped up cream and put it into Jell-O. I'm not sure they thought an English girl would know how to cook. They had probably been feeling sorry for Johnny for being married to an English girl, thinking he didn't have good homemade food to eat. Maybe that was partly why his mom sent home so much food each time he visited.

After dinner, to my surprise and delight, every family gave gifts to Michael because they hadn't given us gifts when he had been born. There were diapers, rattles, and clothes. Again I felt the welcome and love radiating from the entire family with this kind act of generosity. One sister-in-law made Michael dark brown corduroy pants with a beige shirt, and she had it hanging on a little hanger with the suspenders. The pants looked very well made with the clever way she put little snaps up the inner legs. The outfit was so cute that it looked like it had just come out of the store. I had never seen anything like it.

The only awkward part of the day was when Johnny's mom, Saloma, tried to speak English to me. As a true Old Order Amish woman, Saloma's life centered around her home and her family. She didn't get out much, so her English was spotty. Several times she tried to say something in English to me but ended up frustrated, and German words would suddenly come out. Often we ended up just laughing.

Everyone was kind and we enjoyed our visit so much that we stayed there all day. Johnny's sister Susan played a lot with

Michael on his first birthday, in August 1964, at the Ashery Cheese Factory.

Michael and entertained him much of the day, which pleased me and was certainly a welcome relief. When the Amish get together for a holiday, they usually stay all day, enjoying the family times and fellowship. Those who don't have to go home to do chores enjoy a light supper together toward evening.

This day, my first venture into Amish life, left me with satisfaction, and it just confirmed my decision to be Amish. I had found the acceptance and respect, the love and peace that I had longed for my whole life.

When I went to my sister-in-law Lizzie's place again, I asked about the straight pins in the caps. "How do Amish women stand to have those pins in their heads?"

She laughed and laughed. "No, you don't push the pins *into* your scalp! You only catch some hair with the cap."

Did I ever have a lot to learn! Every day I asked Jesus to help me to learn, and he *did* help me! More and more bits of wisdom were given, a little at a time, and more pieces of the puzzle came together. Lucky for me that I didn't have to learn it all at once. Otherwise, who knows what I would have done?

9

An Amish Funeral,
an Amish Birth

I HAD A miscarriage a few months after Michael was born. Two months later, I was pregnant again—or as the Amish used to say, I was "in a family way." Only the English said "pregnant" at that time.

Lizzie thought I should make a black dress next, so that I would be prepared in case something happened to someone in Johnny's family. We didn't know then that Johnny's sister Susan would die two weeks before we had our next baby. But because of Lizzie's help and foresight, the black dress was made and we were prepared.

Johnny's sister Susan knew her health was failing, and she had told me she definitely wanted me to be with the family and at the funeral if something happened to her, even if I was in a family way. Most Amish women back then never went to church or other functions after they were six months along. The Amish women wore bigger and looser dresses than they do now, so that they didn't have to make a different style of dress when they were expecting. Plus, the Amish aprons covered their expanding waistlines.

Johnny and I were living at the Ashery Cheese Factory when the news came of Susan's death. This was during our transition time between English and Amish, and we were still driving our car and truck. On the day of the funeral, we put on our Amish clothes and drove our car to the farm. Out of respect to Johnny's parents, we parked away from the house and barn in a short driveway that led to some woods. From there it was a short walk to their lane and into the farm building where the funeral was held.

All things were done in a very orderly manner during this funeral, as is the Amish custom. As the people began to arrive, they were asked if they planned to go to the cemetery after the service. If the answer was yes, the boys who handled the horses and buggies marked that horse and buggy. A chalk number was placed on the back of the buggy and on the harness of the horse to keep the horses with the right buggy and to denote the order of that buggy in the funeral procession, depending on the owner's age and relationship to the deceased. The boys learn this order as they help with church and funeral services through the years. This knowledge is handed down through hands-on learning, which is a backbone of the Amish community.

In the same fashion, the young girls took the women's black bonnets and kept them in similar order. These black bonnets are used for special occasions and are always worn when an Amish woman is away from home. After the service, the girls knew exactly where each person's bonnet had been stored, and, quietly and without ceremony, returned it to its proper owner. Since it was August and very hot at the time of Susan's funeral, we women just wore our bonnets, but in the winter the Amish women also wear coat and shawl. As I would later learn, it is a requirement for the women always to wear a shawl over the coat. A few of the young girls watched some of the younger children and babies during the service and the procession.

The entire service was organized precisely by a man who worked like a funeral director. This is a position that is handed down from generation to generation. And boy, do they ever know how to keep things in order! During Susan's funeral I was just in awe of the precision and how this director made everything go smoothly with hundreds of people.

While the people were still arriving, Johnny and I joined the other close relatives as they knelt down together for a prayer the bishop held with the family. Then, when the service started, the men and women separated to sit on their own sides of the benches. After the service, everyone gathered around and the funeral director organized the viewing of the body. Everybody came out of the house, and the young girls returned the children to their parents so families could go through the line together. This viewing was done with the closest family members going last, in a kind of reverse order from the funeral procession that would follow. Somehow, even with the hundreds of people standing around, the director made sure every last person went through the viewing line.

After the viewing, the boys lined up the horses and buggies for the procession. First came the hearse, which was a buggy with a long back end to hold the casket. Then the closest relatives—Susan and Johnny's parents—followed. Then came the oldest son, and then the oldest daughter, all down the line and going in order, just as they were numbered by the young men. A young Amish man loaned us a horse and buggy for the funeral procession. Not only had I not ridden in a buggy since my childhood rides with our hired girl's father, I was also pretty big and awkward at eight and a half months pregnant. Imagine how I felt going to my first Amish funeral so far along in my pregnancy!

I was very nervous throughout the day, as it was my first time at an Amish funeral. So much was unfamiliar to me. I was wearing Amish clothes, trying to handle little Michael, who was quite a handful, and experiencing the strangeness of riding in a horse and buggy. Even though Johnny helped by explaining things to me, I still felt like I didn't know what to expect. So I was on pins and needles—which, as I've mentioned before, was not a comfortable feeling. It seemed strange and unsettling to me: strange people, strange ways, a strange method of transportation, and such a sad time at the home. Only God helped me through it all, and I know he helped my husband, too. Johnny drove that horse like he had done it every day since he had left home. Some things never leave a person.

There was quite an involved process with so many horses and buggies to be lined up for the procession, and that made me anxious, too. Horses don't like to stand around long, so they will stamp and get antsy to get going, which also made me nervous as we waited for the procession to start. But the horse we had borrowed was good and held still for us.

It was certainly different for me to see a wooden casket. English people don't typically use undecorated wood for caskets. The strangeness of the day continued for me at the gravesite, as I watched the Amish put rough wood pieces down in the grave. The Amish call this wood "the rough box," but the English call it a "vault." Then the casket was lowered in, and more rough boards were put on top before the dirt was shoveled in.

Although I hadn't known Susan very long, she had made a big impression on my life with her gentle, loving character. She was so in touch with the Lord that he had revealed to her I was going to have a little girl. Before she died on August 22, 1965, Susan had bought a little purse and some toys for a girl.

Our Elizabeth was born a few days later, on September 7. About three weeks after Susan's death, I received the gifts from Susan and a big box of material. She had told my sister-in-law where these things were, should anything happen to her before my due date. God is so awesome.

Some months before my due date, Johnny and I decided to ask our sister-in-law Lizzie and the doctor if I could have a home delivery at Wayne and Lizzie's place. It was much less expensive to have a home delivery—only around three hundred dollars compared to one thousand or more for a hospital delivery. I also had a plan to have Johnny right with me during the delivery, holding my hand and supporting me. At that time Dr. Eberly only did home deliveries for Amish and Mennonite babies. But because I was going to turn Amish, he said yes to the home birth.

On September 7, 1965, blond-haired and blue-eyed Elizabeth was born in Wayne and Lizzie's living room, where Lizzie had put a bed and nightstand in preparation for the birth. Johnny and I had gone there at midnight the night before when my labor started. Because I have such long labors, Johnny went back to the trailer to sleep for the rest of the night. He planned to go to work the next day until we called and told him to come. Throughout my labor I kept thinking how wonderful it was going to be to have him right there with me during the delivery. Around noon when I was about to deliver, we sent Wayne and Lizzie's little boy, Johnny, up over the hill to a phone to call the cheese factory and let my Johnny know it was time to come.

The doctor came and soon the time to deliver was on us, but no Johnny. "What do you want to do?" the doctor asked me. "Do you want to try to wait for Johnny?"

Everyone kept saying, "Johnny will be here in a minute."

Of course I wanted to wait. That was my whole plan. I cried and cried, so disturbed at the impending birth with no husband in sight. But when a baby is coming, there is no holding back. So our precious little girl was born without Johnny beside me. I had so wanted him there, but it was not to be. So much for my idea to have my husband right in the delivery room to hold my hand and give me support!

When Johnny did come after work that day, he was surprised to see our little girl had arrived. His boss's wife had answered the phone, taken the message that I was about to give birth, and forgotten to tell Johnny. So he missed Elizabeth's birth. He sure had something to say to his boss's wife the next day at work.

Lizzie gave Michael and me wonderful care in the week we were there; nobody can take care of you like Lizzie. I was so very happy with our little Elizabeth because I only had brothers. I really loved having a girl, but she was fussy that first day. Lizzie gave her a little water and tried to soothe her, but she didn't calm down. Finally Lizzie said to me, "Put her in your left arm." As soon as I did, little Elizabeth settled right down, and we both slept for a couple of hours. Lizzie said how sweet we both looked sleeping so peacefully together. Praise the Lord!

In that same week we learned that the house next door to Wayne and Lizzie's was for sale. This twelve-acre farm used to be Johnny and Wayne's sister Mattie's place. I was so excited and said, "Next door! Oh my, Johnny, we *have* to buy this place."

True to his character, Johnny didn't say much that night. He went home and slept on it. When he came back the next night, he said, "I'm really going to try to see if we can get that place."

We thought God was opening doors for us and that we had better jump at the chance to get a house in the area where we wanted to live. So five months later we moved from rural Fredericksburg to our Beach City address right next door to Lizzie, who would continue to teach me more about Amish life. I really appreciated all the patience of my husband and Lizzie. I asked a lot of questions, and they never seemed to get tired of answering them.

10

Turning toward a New Way of Life

JOHNNY CONTINUED TO work at the Ashery Cheese Factory under a different owner for another year. We didn't know what kind of job he would be able to get when he joined the Amish church. Fifty years ago, most of the Amish were farmers, although it surely is not like that today.

Soon after the move, I had another miscarriage when I was only two months along. Johnny's blood type is positive and mine is negative, and the doctor said that was part of the reason for the miscarriages. Now that I know more about women's health, I wonder if my eating habits and hormone imbalance might also have had something to do with my miscarriages.

Remember my dream of being married and having six children—three boys and three girls? Well, I had an interesting encounter with an Amish woman one of the first times we attended church. We had started attending with Johnny's parents in the district where we planned to live. On that particular day, church was being held in Johnny's parents' home. After the service, I stood in the dining room making small talk with this woman. "I see your little girl here," I said. "She looks like she is about Michael's age."

She told me when her girl's birthday was—about a week before Michael's—and I said, continuing my small talk, "Oh. How many children do you have?"

"Eleven," she answered.

Immediately she had my attention. "I can't imagine what it would be like to have eleven children!" I exclaimed. In my mind I was thinking that having eleven children would be loads of work, from before sunup to after sundown.

I had no idea then what the future had in store for me.

As happy as Johnny and I were about our decision to turn Amish, not everyone had the same enthusiasm. When I called my mom to tell her the news, her reaction was just as I had expected. "I just knew when you married Johnny that he would turn you Amish."

"No," I said, "he didn't."

"Yes, he did."

"No, he did *not*. This is my decision."

Her next reaction was, "The kids will never have nice clothes." That seemed to be her main concern about me turning Amish.

"Well," I said, "that's just the way it is." Inside I thought, *There's more to life than pretty clothes.* I had told her we were going to be Amish over the phone because I had expected that she would be angry, and I was right. She began ranting and raving until I finally had to hang up. The peace and joy I had felt since God came into my life was worth everything to me. The load of my sin had lifted from my shoulders that day, and God had replaced it with his peace. I wanted to follow him regardless of the cost.

From the time she was born, Elizabeth never wore an English dress. I thought it would be a waste of money to buy her English clothes since we knew we were going to be Amish. Jonas's Fannie made a light pink dress for her, which I thought was really nice. Lizzie also made dresses for Elizabeth, but the ones she made were dark colored.

One of those dresses Lizzie made was dark green. When Michael, Elizabeth, and I went to visit my mom one day, I had put the green dress on Elizabeth. Mom didn't say anything about Elizabeth's dress until I was on the porch, ready to leave. As we were saying our goodbyes, Mom informed me, "If you decide to visit again, you will *not* put that green dress on Elizabeth. I hate green."

I thought just a little bit, and then told her boldly, "Mom, I've got my Lord, my husband, and our family, so I don't need you." After that I turned around and left. This may have seemed harsh, but I felt I had to let her know that my decision to be Amish was made and that Johnny and I were now in charge of our lives.

After weeks of no communication, Mom sent a postcard saying she and Grandma would be coming for a visit. Never a note of sorry or "I said too much." I never heard my mom say she was sorry for anything she had ever said or done. I have always forgiven her, but I also knew I was not going to let her run my life.

When we moved from our trailer to a small house on twelve acres with a barn, I thought I was in a mansion. One of the first things Johnny did was build a hog house and add on to the barn so we could raise hogs in a bigger way.

This little city girl learned to help baby pigs to be born, along with much more about farm life. Can you imagine me, the cheerleader and majorette, holding the hind legs of little boy pigs while Johnny took his sharp knife and castrated them when they were just a few days old? There I'd be, standing and holding tight to those kicking legs while the pig squealed. I could hardly believe it myself. Looking back, I really have to laugh at how dumb I was about farm life and much of life in general.

Three weeks before Mark was born, we took one last vacation to Florida in our 1960 Oldsmobile convertible. We had decided we were ready to join the Old Order Amish church after this baby was a few weeks old. Wayne and Lizzie said we could farm their place of forty-five acres. Wayne was a machinist and they had been leasing their farm, so now that we would be living right by them, they had graciously offered the land for us to work.

After we got back from Florida, we sold our car to a teenager who had been raised Amish but who had not yet joined the church. The first weekend he had it, he totaled that car! We couldn't believe it. "Why would you drive so fast that you would total your brand-new car?" we wondered. I had quit driving long before Johnny did. One day I prayed, "Lord, if you will keep helping me to learn to be Amish, help me not to want to drive anymore." And he did. With two children and no car seats like they have today, I became really nervous about driving.

On May 8, 1967, twenty months after Elizabeth was born, we were blessed with a little boy we named Mark. He was blond and blue-eyed and very contented, just like his sister.

For the first six weeks after a birth, Amish mothers always have a hired girl come and help. These girls work in the home and also do chores if the family has a farm. Since I've had ten children, I've had many hired girls over the years. Sometimes, if each girl could only help for a couple of weeks at a time, I had two or three different helpers after a birth. Many times it was hard to find a girl who could come for as long as six weeks. Some girls worked in factories and couldn't leave their jobs, and many who didn't have outside jobs had other baby cases to help with.

When Mark was three weeks old, we started the process of joining the Amish church. Sitting on hard benches with no backs and holding a three-week-old baby made me very tired and was hard on my back. I always had such a hard time with my back after I had each of my children. It wouldn't be very long into the service before I would have to go into the house and lie on a couch for a little while to give my back a rest. Church started at nine o'clock in the morning and lasted until noon, which seemed long to me. I had never really attended church regularly, and when I had gone, the services were only one or two hours.

I must say that getting the chores done on time and getting to church with three children in a buggy was quite a chore. Thinking back now, I don't know how I made it. But I was very willing to follow the Lord's leading and do my best. I would braid Elizabeth's hair on Saturday night and put a handkerchief on her head, hoping I wouldn't have to redo it Sunday morning because I knew I wouldn't have time.

The Amish only have church every two weeks, but may go to neighboring churches in between if they like. Much of the time, Johnny and I used that off-week to stay home and rest. With Johnny working long hours on the farm and often at an outside job as well, this was our one day to really see each other and talk together.

———————

The hardest part of turning Amish for me was learning the language. I got some German spelling books and spent a couple of days teaching myself the ABCs—the "Ah-Bay-Says," as the Amish say them. There were pictures in this book, so I learned the nouns fairly quickly. But those few days were all the time that I, a mother with three children and lots of farmwork on top of the housework and childcare, could spare. The pronouns and verbs were not so easy, and I never did get to where I could speak German fluently and easily.

Johnny and Lizzie helped me with the sounds. At first I didn't realize that when Johnny spoke to the children in Pennsylvania German, I was repeating to myself what he said. Listening to him and repeating, I learned to understand the language. He talked in German to the children and in English to me, so our children were bilingual right from birth. Michael didn't learn to talk really well until he was three, but when he did talk, he knew both languages right down the middle. People couldn't believe he could speak two languages before he went to school. Typically Amish families speak only German at home, so the children speak only German until they go to school. That makes it a little difficult for them when they begin to attend school.

To this day, I still speak English, even to all my Amish friends, although I understand German. Some people have asked me why I don't speak German, since I've now been Amish for almost fifty years. I guess I just didn't take the time to study and learn the verbs and the sentence order. I can speak the nouns and the verbs, but the order is so different that I can't make myself understood. I have the same problem with the songs. When they are translated into English, the words are not in the same order.

I do understand Pennsylvania German, but when the preacher stands up and reads from the Bible, that is all in High German, which is harder for me to understand, especially if the preacher speaks or reads fast. Many Amish tell me, "Oh, don't worry. We agree with you. We don't even understand all those words." I've heard that many times, so I don't feel badly about having trouble with the High German.

All these years, I have conversed with the Amish in English, and they either speak English or German back to me. I did speak some Pennsylvania German to the kids when they were little, and they understood me just fine. But when they got a little older, they laughed at me, and announced to the others, "Did you hear Mom? She didn't say that word right. Hee, hee, hee!" There came a point where they could speak German much better than me, and they could roll their r's, which I never could do very well.

Sometimes when I speak a little German to people, they will say, "Yeah, I know what you said, but you don't have the accent."

"Well, sorry," I will say. "As long as you understood what I said." Encounters like this don't encourage me to keep speaking German.

Even with Johnny, my trials haven't been met with success. If I speak a little German to Johnny, a lot of times he doesn't pay any attention to me. So I'll say, "Okay, when I talk German to you, you don't pay any attention to me. Do I have to say it in English?" He is so used to speaking English to me, he just can't look at me and talk German. I guess he can't really hear me unless I speak English to him.

———————

Another big adjustment in learning to live Amish was not having electricity. We only had electricity for six months after we were baptized, so I never had a refrigerator in the house next to Wayne and Lizzie, just an icebox. Using an icebox was really different. Although we had an icebox when I was very little, I didn't really remember using it and didn't know how it worked. I was so little, I never paid any attention except to get my piece of ice when the iceman came in the summer. I also had a kerosene cooking stove. Some of my sisters-in-law had clear gas stoves, but I refused to have one because I was so scared of them. With the kerosene stove I simply turned up the wick and lit it, and there was no "poofing" of gas.

It was that little "poof" explosion of gas, which often happened when they were lit, that kept me from using our clear gas lamps. For almost two years, I used a kerosene lamp to read in the evening because I was scared that the gas might explode if I tried to light one of our gas lamps. I was also afraid of burning my fingers, because we only had the little matches or the slightly longer wooden ones in the boxes. There was no such thing as a torch to light the lamps or stove. Even those longer stick matches burned down so quickly and almost burned my fingers when I lit the generator valve on the gas lantern. I soon learned that when I held my match to the generator to heat it up first, the generator didn't "poof" as much when I lit it. But boy, each time I had to light the gas lamp I was sure it would explode.

At night when it became darker in the house, I would think, *Oh, no, I'm not going to even try to light that gas lamp.* The kids and I sat at the library table in the evenings, which had an oil lamp, and I read to them. Finally someone showed me a propane torch that I could use to light the gas lamps. This was so much easier, because it was longer and it didn't burn out so quickly. I didn't have to worry about burning my fingers since they were well away from the flame, and it stayed lit until the gas caught. Using the torch, I finally learned how to light the gas lamps and began using them often. Eventually I became brave enough that I could even light them with wooden matches.

Probably one of the worst things about becoming Amish was all the motors. I have never, *ever* liked the noise of a motor. I hated to hear them run, especially the washing machine motor. We didn't have generators when we first became Amish. We had an air-compressor motor outside, and we had the washing machine motor inside. The noise of the air compressor was very bad, but the noise of the washing machine was even worse. And then there were the fumes. The two-cycle Briggs and Stratton motor on the washing machine had an exhaust pipe that sometimes cracked, and then I had fumes right inside where I washed. I got terrible headaches from breathing fumes while I washed when the exhaust was cracked.

So here I was, making all these adjustments and learning to be Amish. I was a wife and mother of three children, and I was learning to sew all our clothes, manage a garden, farm on a small scale, and can fruits, vegetables, and meat. There was a lot to learn for a twenty-three-year-old city girl. I even learned to milk by hand, although I could never match my husband's milking skills. He could really milk well!

11

Baptismal Victory in Jesus

IN THE FALL of 1967, four years and three children after my conversion at the kitchen sink, Johnny and I were to be baptized into the Amish faith. Finally we were joining the church. When a person joins the Amish church, he or she goes to nine instruction classes. These classes are held two times each year for anyone wanting to join. If it happens that nobody is joining at that time, no classes are held. The bishop knew how many years we had wanted to join, and how many years we had been preparing, so he asked the other preachers if they would approve of us taking only eight classes instead of the usual nine. When they agreed, they asked all the church members, who also agreed, because we understood the Amish faith and practices so well by that time.

A day or two before someone is going to get baptized, the elders of the church get together with the candidates and ask them again, "Do you really want to join the Amish church?" "Do you want to give your life to the Lord like this?" They want to make sure that people are joining of their own desire and that no one is forcing them to do it. This was exactly the case with Johnny and me: we were freely choosing to join.

It's finally here, I thought on the morning of our baptism, September 9. I had waited, prayed, and planned almost four years for this day. Joy and a sense of completion filled my heart as I carefully put on my black church dress, white cape, and white apron. I looked fully Amish. After this day, I would *be* fully Amish, embracing this way of life for the rest of my life.

Our baptism was at Wayne and Lizzie's. When they first found out we wanted to be Amish, they said, "Oh, we want the baptism to be at our place." Wayne and Lizzie were so inspirational to our joining the Amish church that we wanted our baptism to be held at their place, too. Church was held in the top of their barn, where they kept the hay and straw. That is where many Amish hold church, not in the bottom of the barn where all the stock is. A day or two before church, the *Gma Bunk Vauga* (church bench wagon) comes, and the man of the house and any other men or boys available set up all the benches for the church service. These benches are wooden with foldable legs, for compact storage, and are all different lengths, from four feet up to ten feet, to make use of the space.

The Old Order Amish church service is very orderly, just like the funeral we attended for Johnny's sister. Before church starts, the women file in by age and then the men do the same, with the women on the left and the men on the right. Everybody sits down and starts singing the first song. On the second line of the song, the bishop stands up and files out, followed by the other preachers. Anyone who is going to be joining the church follows. The oldest man or boy stands up first, then the next oldest, and so on, followed by the women or girls in order by age. But with our circumstances—the fact that we were already married—the young man who was joining with us, Atlee

Schlabach, went first. Then came Johnny, and then came me. Even though Johnny was the oldest man, Johnny had told Atlee that he could go first so Johnny could sit beside me during our joining and the baptism.

We went into a room in Wayne and Lizzie's house for about a half hour of instruction. The bishop did most of the teaching, with the other preachers contributing. When our instruction for the morning was over, the bishop and preachers filed out and spoke together for a little bit, while those of us being instructed went out to the church meeting. After a while, the preachers continued the church service.

On our joining day, everybody was on their benches, ready for church before nine o'clock as usual. Wayne cared for our son and Lizzie took care of little Elizabeth and baby Mark that day, as they had all the times we had gone into the *Abrote* (instruction). Wayne had always had a soft place in his heart for Michael, but he also made Michael behave. Even though Lizzie was at least ten to twelve years older than me, I sat up by her, not in my order, until some time went by and we were members of the church. Then we found our rightful place. Our kids always wanted to sit with Lizzie because they were used to her. She had wanted a whole passel of children, but it just didn't happen. Often Michael went to sit with Uncle Wayne because he always had gum or candy for him.

Bishop Isaac Miller was there for the baptism. He is a slow speaker, so the service went a long, long time that day. We didn't get baptized until one thirty or two o'clock in the afternoon, and I was getting pretty hungry by that time. When Bishop Miller was finished, we knelt down in front of our benches on the front row, ready to receive the baptism. I had read all about what we had to do on the day of our baptism, because I wanted to be very prepared. Even though I didn't understand everything they were saying in the service, I was thinking of all I had read and learned, so I could follow along in my heart.

They asked, "Do you still believe?"

We said, "*Ya, ich glaube es Jesus Christus Gottes Sonne isht*" (Yes, I believe Jesus Christ is the Son of God). I was prepared for that and answered in German, because I wanted to say it right.

Lizzie came forward to untie the strings and remove my *Kapp*. Usually one of the oldest women comes forward to hold the *Kapp* for any woman being baptized. But this morning, it was Lizzie who came forward to take my cap off and hold it, even though she was not the oldest. She had told the oldest of the women, "I want to be the one who is going to hold her *Kapp*. I want to be the one who takes her hand and gives the kiss of Christ on her cheek." She insisted, because she had helped me learn and prepare for this all those years.

"I baptize you in the name of the Father and the Son and the Holy Spirit," Bishop Miller said as the water was poured on our heads from a cup. Then he took Johnny's hand and gave him the kiss of Christ. Turning to me, he also took my hand, welcoming me into the Amish community. Lizzie then took my hand, gave me the kiss, and put my *Kapp* back on my head. Tears began to spill out of our eyes as Johnny and I took our seats.

Even though the Amish are not usually emotional, we just had to cry. So many years we had worked and prayed and studied for this day. We sat there and cried—cried for joy, joy in the Lord. Our hearts and our eyes were flowing over, knowing all the years and all the trials we had gone through to accomplish this.

After our baptism, church was over and we had a satisfying lunch. The bishop said something to Lizzie, and she came and said to Johnny, "They want to take you into the instruction room to give you the instructions for a couple getting married, because you weren't married in the Amish church."

"Oh," I said. "I see." So off we went to the instruction room again. This instruction was about the permanence of marriage, about the roles and order in the home. Although I didn't understand much of what they were saying because I hadn't prepared for this instruction time, Johnny told me later what they had said. I really hadn't understood everything in our other instruction times either, because I didn't fully understand the language. But each time I went home and read about it, and then I knew. Lizzie also filled me in. She would ask me, "Did they tell you this?" as things came to mind, and that also helped me to realize more about my role as an Amish wife.

The only bad part of the day was when some woman said to Lizzie, "Do you think Marlene and Johnny already regret they got baptized?"

"What in the world do you mean?" Lizzie asked. She was shocked that someone would think this, let alone say it, especially on the very day of our baptism.

"Well, because they sat there crying," the woman said.

I was floored! How could anybody say that? Four years Johnny and I had been living English, Amish, English, Amish, and the last many months we had been strictly Amish.

I have said for years that some people just don't fully understand the good news of Jesus or grasp the meaning behind being baptized. The depth of what the Lord did for us and is doing for us is astounding. Maybe people couldn't realize how deeply we felt that day—how our emotions were overflowing to see this change in our lives come to fulfillment. They didn't know how deeply we were feeling what Jesus had done for us.

When I made the decision to be Amish, I was also considering the future of my family, not just myself. Life wasn't just about me anymore. Johnny and I already had three children before our baptism finally took place. Part of my decision to become Amish was about Johnny and our children: Michael, Elizabeth, and Mark. Having a family made me more open and responsive to the Lord's teaching. Until I had children I didn't understand how deeply I would care for each child and the great responsibility I would feel for their upbringing and moral development. I had a much broader view of what Jesus Christ did and how his grace applied to me, and I wanted that for our children. On our baptism day Johnny and I were full of the love that we had for Jesus, the love that we had for each other and our family, and the love we had for the church.

This was "the day which the Lord hath made." We rejoiced and were glad in it! Jesus won a victory the day I was converted. He won the day Johnny and I were baptized. Throughout our lives we must always contemplate the cross and not miss the glory of it. What other man died upon such a cruel tree yet now lives? Like the women at the empty tomb, I want to tell others of his victory and our victory. "Because I live, ye shall live also," Jesus promised us (John 14:19). Thanks be to God, who "giveth us the victory through our Lord Jesus Christ" (1 Corinthians 15:57).

A couple of weeks after we were baptized, Lizzie said to us, "I want to have an Amish wedding dinner for you."

"What?" I said. We'd been married for four years, so what was the big deal about having a wedding dinner now? She had mentioned this before, but I thought, *It won't happen. We didn't really have much of a wedding anyway. Who cares about a wedding dinner?*

Lizzie said, "Yes, I am having an Amish wedding dinner for you. I'd be so happy to do this, considering you didn't have a very nice English wedding." She also said, "There's going to be lots of food and hopefully presents."

She insisted, and the wedding dinner was planned for the second Saturday in September at Wayne and Lizzie's. She got her house all ready and set up lots of tables in the dining room and living room.

Johnny's sisters Mattie, Fannie, and Elizabeth and sisters-in-law Anna, Verna, and of course Lizzie and I helped prepare the food on Friday. It took most of the day to prepare the food: celery, carrots, potatoes, and toasting the bread for dressing; chicken, mashed potatoes, dressing, gravy, and a vegetable plate; and lots of pies, cakes, and date pudding. Lizzie was right: I could see it from the overflowing tables. There *is* a lot of food at an Amish wedding dinner.

The day for our wedding dinner arrived bright and sunny, and with excitement in the air in our house I wore the new, dark blue dress I had worn for joining the church. I chose that dress because most Amish girls wear dark blue for their wedding days. Johnny wore his church suit and white shirt with black shoes. And of course I had on my white *Kapp*.

Johnny and I were the first to be seated, and we sat in the *Eck* (corner) to the right of the living room door. The wedding party usually sits in a corner at a special table, and with them sit what the English would call their attendants. Lizzie, in her usual loving way, said we could have whomever we wanted, but she suggested that I might like Johnny's cousin Amanda sitting as my bridesmaid *niebe* (next to) me, since there would be no English people at the dinner. I readily agreed, because Amanda Schlabach Yoder was very special to me and I to her. She was so thrilled I had turned from English to Amish. Amanda went through many trials in her marriage, and she was so godly. She had no children and her husband had left the Amish church but continued to live with her. These days, the groom usually picks a boy and girl to sit beside him and the bride picks a boy and a girl to sit beside her.

After Johnny and I were seated with our attendants, the rest of the Amish relatives and friends filed in to their places. Tears came to our eyes as we saw the abundance of delicious food. Here was a meal fit for a king and a queen. The wedding cakes Lizzie had for us—two angel food cakes side by side on a nice big board—were frosted with seven-minute frosting and decorated with walnuts, with a light-blue ribbon and bow tied in front. I thought they looked like two wedding rings side by side.

It was such a peaceful and serene time that we could feel the presence of the Lord in the room. After the meal and singing some German songs, we opened presents. Lizzie had given people suggestions for things we needed. We got towels, sheet sets, kitchen utensils, serving bowls and glasses, small hand tools, and someone even gave us a high chair with folding steps that Michael and Elizabeth loved to sit on. I was very happy for it. We ended up having that chair for so long that all our children used it. Some of the uncles and aunts gave us money, and there was dress material for me and Elizabeth and toys for the children.

After four years of marriage and three children, I had given up all thought of getting wedding gifts. But here we were, finally receiving wedding gifts! We felt so blessed that day to have all these relatives come and celebrate with us. We were very, very touched by it, and we gave many thanks to Wayne and Lizzie.

Johnny's relatives and our new Amish friends welcomed us into their community, and they were in our hearts. The warm feeling of family and belonging just reinforced what I already knew: being Amish was right for me.

12

Mini-Farm Adventures

WE BOUGHT A small herd of six Guernsey cows from an English neighbor and started farming at Wayne's place about the time Mark was born. Johnny went down to chore in the morning, and I sometimes went along in the evening.

On our own place of twelve acres we had chickens, sows (pregnant female pigs), hogs (pigs of either gender raised for butchering for meat), pigs (the babies), dogs, and cats.

Raising pigs was the real introduction into farming for this city girl. If the sows got out of their pen when Johnny was at work, which they often did, it was my job to round them up and get them back in. The reason the sows got out of their pen was to go eat the other sows' pigs. Once they got a taste of pig meat, they wanted that more than anything. They even started eating their own pigs. Johnny said the sow that caused us the most problems was crazy. I spent many hours chasing that sow all over the field, trying to get her back where she belonged. But when she heard the sound of Johnny's truck, she hightailed it for home. As Johnny drove down the hill, he could see the sow jump over a high woven wire fence and get back in the pen. I might have been chasing it for an hour, trying to get it back into the pen. But she knew the sound of Johnny's truck and knew there was trouble ahead if she wasn't in her pen when he got home, so home she ran.

Johnny worked hard at farming, and he just loved it. The kids and I helped all we could. But after farming for about one year, Johnny decided he had to get another job to supplement our income. We kept going into debt to the feed mill, because we didn't have enough acreage to raise all the grain we needed to keep our family afloat. So Johnny started an afternoon shift at a window-and-door plant in a nearby town. With our growing family and so little land, he had to do something to make ends meet.

After Johnny started working away from the farm, we sold all the cows except one. He knew I couldn't trudge with all the children down our lane and up the road to Wayne's barn every evening to take care of the cows. We brought our remaining cow up to the small barn on our little farm, where we also kept our horse.

Johnny built on the back of the barn so we could raise hogs to butchering size. We raised hundreds of hogs on that small place. We sold most of them, but we also butchered a couple each year and put the meat in a locker in town, where it was kept frozen. We cut up the shoulder meat into little chunks that I used in sauerkraut. We also had hams and bacon, which we put in salt brine and then smoked. We brined the bacon a shorter time than it took for ham. Ham has to brine six to eight weeks clear into the bone, or it will rot. We also smoked link sausage.

Michael was really a boy through and through, and he was bossy! He was always telling Elizabeth what to do and where to go. If she didn't listen he pounded on her back to try to force her. He had to be spanked many times for hurting her.

But Elizabeth also had a strong will of her own. When she was around three she started riding the tricycle in the middle of the road because our sidewalk was so steep. She rode out there a dozen times or more a day. This was a very busy and dangerous road. She could have been killed riding out there, so I had to spank her many times for doing this. But she still persisted. At three years old, she probably couldn't understand how important it was not to ride in the road.

One day I heard the coal trucks coming down the road, and they seemed to stop in front of our house. I hurried to the front to look. Sure enough, there was Elizabeth, this tiny little girl on her little trike, out on the road between two large coal trucks. I heard one driver say to the other one, "Make sure to always watch very carefully here, because this little girl likes to ride her trike on the road."

After working in a field across from our house, I went in to make lunch one day. I had the shock of my life when I walked into the kitchen. Elizabeth, who was at least three, was sitting on the countertop with an empty bottle of baby aspirin. A butter knife, which she had used to pry off the lid, lay beside her. After taking a deep breath to control my emotions, I calmly said to her, "Elizabeth, did you eat all those pills?"

She answered, just as calmly, "Yes."

"Why did you eat those pills?"

She answered so innocently, "I was hungry, hungry, *hungry.*"

After I got the bottle away from her and saw that every pill was gone, I ran back out to the porch and yelled to Johnny in the field across the road from the house. "Elizabeth ate all the baby aspirin! It was a full bottle. Now what should we do?"

In his own calm way, Johnny said, "Well, I'll go and call for a driver to take her to the doctor." I guess he figured this was not something we could deal with on our own. Once we were at the doctor's, they had to pump her stomach. When they tried to put a tube down her nose into her stomach, Elizabeth just cried and cried. She cried so much that she threw up at least four times. When they finally did get the tube in, they really weren't able to get anything pumped out because she had thrown up so much.

Even to this day, it's hard for me to believe a child that young could get that childproof lid off. Many times I have pried and pried, trying to get one of those lids off. As I said, she is one determined girl.

When we did chores down the road at Wayne's, Johnny carried Mark and one five-gallon bucket of ear corn down to the barn. When Mark was big enough to crawl, Johnny put him in the empty bucket for the ride home. Mark loved to squeeze himself into the bucket, kneeling down with his little head peeking out, and his little hands on the rim of the bucket. He was so cute, and he reminded me of a little coon poking himself up out of a hole. Mark looked forward to that ride with his daddy every evening.

After our first summer on the farm, we finally had wheat and oats we could thresh with the threshing machine. I didn't even know what a threshing machine did, and when I saw how it worked, I was amazed at how it could separate the grain from the straw. Our fields were so small that it didn't take the men long to thresh, so I didn't have to make a meal for them. I would just set up drinks and some snacks on a card table for the workers to grab on their way to the next farm. I remember thinking, *Oh, I could never make a threshing meal like my sisters-in-law make for all those men.* When I went to help my other sister-in-law, Anna, occasionally, I saw all the food she had to prepare for all the men and boys who came. It took us all day and more to get it all ready. Cooking that much extra food, on top of what was needed daily for our growing family, seemed like a big deal to me.

That year, Johnny quit working the afternoon shift and started the day shift at L-P in Winesburg. He also worked part-time at Winesburg Meats. Thank goodness he was so healthy and could continue his heavy workload. I wasn't so lucky. I was always sick and tired. Every winter I made three or four trips to the doctor for pills or cough syrup. Back then, I knew little about nutrition, and I think now it surely didn't help for me to be making—and eating—all those pies, cookies, and cakes so often.

Later on, after we moved to a one-hundred-acre farm, I planned and made large meals for workers who came for a threshing, a shed raising, silo fillings, as well as weddings, church, and a funeral at our place. I'm thankful I couldn't see into the future in those early days. Knowing what was before me might have overwhelmed me.

When Mark was eleven months and three weeks old, we had a little girl named Malinda on May 2, 1968. Johnny had an Aunt Malinda who looked just like his mother, and like her she was always smiling. It used to be common for the Amish to name their children after relatives, but it is not as common with the younger generation.

About a month before Malinda was born, a tragic accident happened to my brother Garry near Perry Heights by Massillon. A seventeen-year-old girl turned left at a traffic light and didn't

see him coming on his motorcycle. The impact was so hard he
flew as high as the electrical wires and crashed on the road. His
helmet flew off, and he was injured badly. He lived for a couple
of days in a coma and then died on April 1, 1968.

Garry had always been good to me. Everybody said Garry
and I looked like our dad, while the other children in our family
looked like Mom. I felt especially close to him because of this
resemblance and because of his character. Garry was so kind
to our little brother, Greg, which made Greg really love him,
too. Garry bought Greg everything he could that Greg asked
for, things our parents couldn't afford: a swing set, a tricycle,
a bicycle, and a rocking horse. Greg would ask, "Could I have
this, please?" And Garry would say, "Okay, I'll get it for you as
soon as I can afford it."

Losing Garry was difficult for me. I had so many emotions
inside, because I wasn't sure he was saved. That just tore me
apart. While he was still alive I went to visit him in the hospital,
and as I stood there next to his broken body, I prayed for him,
"God, have mercy on him." I cried and cried, and I prayed and
prayed, but saw no reaction from him. My heart was broken,
wanting mercy from God, wanting the best for him.

A nurse came in, saw my grief, and said sarcastically, "What
is he to you?"

I said, "He's my brother." Noting my Amish dress, she looked
at me up and down in disbelief. Maybe she had a hard time
believing an Amish woman could be related to this non-Amish
young man.

When I came out of the room, I said to my mom, "Oh my,
I just wish he would live, and if he does, that he would live for
Jesus Christ."

She said, "What do you mean? He was the nicest boy."

Although he was on life support for two or three days, Garry never regained consciousness.

One year after my brother Garry died, Johnny's mother, Saloma, died at age seventy-three. After Johnny's sister Susan died, it seemed Saloma's health really went downhill. The doctors found she had hardening of the arteries, and she fell down the basement steps several times. She also began having trouble with her speech and could hardly talk during her last months here on earth. One day when Johnny's father, Andy, came in from the shop, he found Saloma kneeling in front of the couch. She was gone. Andy found her there on her knees to pray her last prayer to the Lord. Amen!

Saloma and I always had a very wonderful relationship after I came to her home that first Thanksgiving. Even though she could not speak much English, we really tried hard to communicate with each other, especially because Johnny wanted me to learn to bake like his mom. We had many wonderful times cooking together during those early days. Saloma would speak some English when getting the ingredients ready, but she would soon forget herself and start talking German. We had many a laugh about that.

Saloma was so soft-spoken, kind, and gentle. I really loved her. Johnny said he never heard his mother complain, and she smiled almost all the time. She was just a smiler. Not that she had an easy life. She had three diabetic children whom she buried at young ages: Clyde, who died at twenty-nine; Eli, who was blind and who died at thirty-four; and Susan, who died at thirty-one. They all had deep, deep sores that she had to dress and care for every night—night after night, day after day, from the time they were four years old.

Johnny's parents were not physically affectionate with their children as the children got older, but Johnny definitely knew he was loved. He often talked to me about his parents and their love for him. That was a big part of what drew me to him, his being so touched by his parents' love. He said, "They never had to tell me they loved me every day, nothing like that. I just knew."

Acknowledging what a wonderful woman Johnny's mother was, I told him once, "I will never be like her. You might as well face it now." For one thing, I had a fiery temper. On both my mom's and dad's sides of the family I had Welsh and Irish blood, so I figured I came by it honestly! My temper came quickly, but also faded quickly. My mom's anger was much slower to die down, sometimes lasting a week or two. When I was young and noticed her weeks of anger and silence, I thought, *If I ever get married, I'm not staying angry that long.* And I have done my best to keep to that promise, even though I could never live up to Saloma's wonderful temperament.

I remember taking a meal to Saloma and Andy the last winter she was alive. I made sloppy joes, bread-and-butter pickles, homemade cake, and ice cream. During the meal I kept asking Saloma if she liked everything and if it tasted good enough for her. She was so weak then she could only smile and nod her head. Losing her was such a loss for Johnny and me, but I knew heaven had a new jewel there.

In June 1968 my dearest and beloved Grandma Smith died on the couch in her dining room. That dining room had precious memories for me, because that's where our family had often gathered for Thanksgiving dinner, waiting to eat the turkey we always got from the newspaper company as a gift because my brothers and I peddled newspapers. From the time I was nine until I was twelve, I stayed at Grandpa and Grandma's for one week during the summer. Those were such carefree, happy times with my grandma, whom I loved so much. She made one lemon pie just for me during those stays because I loved it, and she told me I could only have one piece each day, as more wouldn't be good for me. She did many special things for me, like taking me to Massillon on the Greyhound bus to buy a new pair of Buster Brown shoes. She bought those shoes one or two sizes too big to make them last, putting cardboard inside so I could wear them until I grew into them. I loved watering her garden and even using her push mower to mow her grass. When I turned Amish, that experience came back to me when I used a push mower to mow our yard.

All these precious memories flooded my mind as I mourned my dear relatives. This was a sad time, and I felt almost lost without them.

———————

I was always beside Johnny, helping him out in the field, before our children were old enough to take my place. We were a team; we did everything together.

Once when I was helping Johnny build a fence along the road, he said, "Go put some kerosene in a jar and bring it here. I want to burn a little brush along this fence."

Michael and Elizabeth were outside by us, and Mark was nearby, too, toddling around. He was just a little over a year old. I brought the kerosene, and as Johnny finished burning the brush, he set the jar of kerosene on a fence post. Mark looked at that jar and said, "*Wasser*" (water). He must have been thirsty and thought it looked like water.

We told him, "*Nay, net Wasser. Du daufst net hava. Das bache*" (That's not water. You can't have that. It's yucky). And we continued working.

He kept urging, "*Wasser.*"

"No, you can't have that. It's kerosene, *bache.*"

Johnny told Michael to go put the kerosene up in a storage cabinet outside the basement, where no one could get into it. A little later, I said, "I'm taking Mark in. He needs a nap." I thought, *I'll just lay him on the couch for his nap instead of putting him in his bed.* So I laid him down with his bottle and went back out to help Johnny finish our fence.

About an hour later, I stopped and lifted my head, listening. *What is that noise? It sounds like a little child coughing. Who is coughing?*

After a few minutes, the noise continued. Something told me to go check it out, so I ran over to the basement. There was Mark with the jar of kerosene standing beside him, oil running out of his mouth.

"Oh no," I cried, terror rising within me. "He drank the kerosene!"

Johnny came running and took Mark to lay him out on the lawn. Mark's eyes started going back in his head, and I panicked. "Oh, oh, oh. We've got to get help, we've got to get help!" I yelled. Johnny picked Mark up and carried him into the back of our kitchen.

"Just calm down. He's still breathing. Let's see what Wayne says." To my amazement Johnny left me there with Mark while he went down to consult with his brother at his farm.

Meanwhile Mark was gasping, trying to breathe, as if his lungs were filling. *Oh, I can't wait*, I thought. *Air, he needs air!* I picked him up, ran out the door, and laid him again on the grass, fanning him, wondering how long Johnny would be gone. *What am I going to do? What am I going to do?* I felt helpless watching my baby struggle to breathe and not knowing what I could do to help him.

Finally, after what seemed an interminably long time, Johnny came back with Wayne.

Frustrated, I said, "What is going on?" My voice was tense with pent-up anxiety.

"Oh, he'll get better. Don't be so concerned," Wayne calmly said. I thought, *Easy for you to say not to be concerned. This is not your kid!*

In a short time, Mark started throwing up. He threw up and threw up—lots of kerosene. It seemed the crisis had passed, and we hoped that the kerosene was out of his system. Later, as I thought about the events leading up to this accident, I said suddenly, "Do you realize what we saved him with? His bottle. He had just had a bottle of milk." I realized that the milk mixing with the kerosene had caused him to throw up.

The next day, when Mark was still rasping and not breathing right, I said firmly, "I'm going to take him to the doctor." Usually I got Johnny's approval before taking this drastic measure, but this was one time I was determined to get help for my baby.

After the doctor checked Mark out thoroughly, he said, "It's a wonder this boy is still alive. I can hear the kerosene rattling in his lungs. He could have gotten pneumonia."

Then he added, "Try to keep the kerosene out of reach of little babies." We told him how it had happened, how we had asked our son to put it up out of reach. He advised us what to watch for and gave us some medication, and Mark recovered.

———————

Back then, Amish women used to go to each other's houses to help the family hosting church to get ready. A family usually hosted church once a year. If they didn't have a big barn, they just hosted church in the summer. The closest neighbors and relatives, usually around eight to ten women, came for a whole day, and they helped cook food, helped with the chores, and got the yards and gardens ready. Now the women don't often go over and spend a day helping. They just make pies or cookies to bring for the meal. Thank the Lord people came to help me when we hosted church, or I don't know how I would have been able to manage. I had so many outside chores to do with the farm that I couldn't get my home ready without help.

One time, I planned to help a neighbor down the road get ready for church. I told Johnny I was going to take the horse and our new buggy to the neighbor's house and then to Wilmot afterward to get some groceries. When the work was done at the neighbor's house, I got ready to leave, and the hired girl there hitched up my horse. I didn't notice that she hooked one of the lines onto the halter instead of the bridle. When I was going down the lane, I thought, *My horse is acting funny with its head.* That's when I noticed that one of the lines was hooked to the halter.

I got off and got the line hooked onto the bridle. Then I started to get into the buggy, still holding on to the lines across the horse's back. This horse had been a racehorse, and I knew he wouldn't stand still very long, so I was trying to hurry and get on before he took off. I wasn't very skilled at this whole horse-and-buggy thing, yet. Just as I took one step into the buggy, that horse took off.

Oh, no! I determined. *You're not ruining this new buggy. I've waited too many years to get this buggy.* So I kept hold of the lines, running beside the buggy, until my feet were just flying out from under me. Then the horse started dragging me. But I was just as determined as the horse, so I gritted my teeth and held on tight. I was not going to let that horse ruin my new buggy.

Then, when I remembered that I was expecting a baby, I realized I'd better let go. So I did, and the horse just kept on going. Our neighbors saw the horse and buggy going down the road and thought, *Gee, it doesn't look like there's anybody in the buggy!* The horse went up to the crossroad, turned right, continued on the road and made a left at the next crossroad, came down, and stopped in front of our big barn. That's where Johnny always pulled up to unhitch the horse.

Some of our kids ran out to see me, expecting I had just come from the store.

"There's no Mom," they yelled in dismay as they reached the buggy and saw it empty. "No Mom!"

"Dad, Dad!" they hollered to Johnny out in the field. "There's no Mom in our buggy!"

In the meantime, two men who had also been helping at the neighbor's house saw what had happened. They jumped into their horse and buggy to try to follow my runaway horse, but he was so fast they couldn't even keep up with him. When they arrived at our place, there was the horse, still hooked up and standing in front of the barn.

By that time Johnny had come from the field and was there by the horse, because the kids were screaming. So the men explained to Johnny and the kids what had happened. Then the men asked, "What should we do? We know Marlene needed to go to the store." One of them said, "I'll jump in her buggy and take it back to her." When he brought it back to me, I went downtown and did my grocery shopping without any more problems.

So I have never really been comfortable with driving a horse and buggy. I always tried to be very alert, as anything can happen to the buggy or the horse. Something can tear on a harness, the buggy can upset on uneven ground, or any number of things. So I could never fully relax. It seemed things always happened when I drove, but not when Johnny drove.

⸺⸺⸺⸺⸺⸺

In the fall of 1969, on September 6, we were blessed again with another baby, a brown-haired, brown-eyed little boy, whom we named Wayne after Johnny's brother. I'll never forget that labor. It took three days. When the doctor finally came, the baby still delayed for some hours. The doctor went to our grape arbor and ate grapes until the nurse told him, "She's ready now."

I didn't blame the doctor one little bit for going out and eating our grapes. I was tired of waiting, too. I wished I could have been out there with him eating grapes—even though I didn't like grapes. I wished I could do anything but the hard labor I was enduring.

I was so exhausted after that long labor that I told my hired girl to take care of the baby the first night. I decided not to even try to nurse him, because I never could nurse any of the others. Wayne cried as soon as his eyes were open, and did that until he was three or four years old, but he was the best little boy in church. Johnny said he hardly knew Wayne was sitting beside him at church because he was so quiet. It seemed he cried at every little thing, and as he grew we noticed he liked things very neat and orderly. He often got frustrated when he was little because things weren't to his satisfaction. "My spoon isn't right," he would wail, refusing to eat until it was correct. He loved horses and loved playing with beads as though he was driving a horse. He liked horses so much, Johnny sometimes caught him standing beside the big workhorses and petting their hind legs. I'll never know how he avoided being kicked. An angel must have been watching over him.

───

As if I didn't have enough to do with the children, care of the garden and house, and all the chores, I also took care of laying hens and washed eggs every day to make a little bit more money. I sold the eggs for thirty cents a dozen. Some of my English neighbors thought thirty cents was too much and tried to dicker me down, but I didn't budge. I knew how much the feed cost and how hard I had worked for each dozen. No way was I going to sell them any cheaper.

In the fall of 1970, the day before Wayne turned one, Susan was born on September 5. The doctor didn't make it in time because he decided to have another cup of the coffee his wife had made him that morning. He remembered how my labor with Wayne had taken three days, and thought there was no hurry.

So Johnny delivered Susan about five o'clock in the morning, while the children slept upstairs. They never heard a thing and didn't know our new baby had arrived until we told them. Susan was named after Johnny's sister and a distant cousin of mine, who was blond and blue-eyed just like our Susan. Susan was a very contented baby, a welcome blessing.

13

On the Verge of Leaving

JOHNNY FARMED during the day, ran into the house to eat a late lunch, and rushed off to be at work by three o'clock in the afternoon. He was scheduled to work until eleven o'clock at night, but many afternoons they asked if he could work overtime. Since we needed the money, he felt he couldn't say no, so he often worked until seven in the morning. Then he came home and started farming again, hoping to get some sleep on Saturdays and the in-between Sunday if we didn't go to church. What a life that was! We lived that way for two years. Johnny aged ten years in those two years because of lack of sleep. Since then, with proper nutrition, however, he is often taken for being ten years younger than he actually is.

Those years were so very hard on both of us, and how I kept from going insane at that time God only knows. I remember in the evenings the children and I sat on the porch swing and sang. We would just sing and swing. There were many nights I also cried because I wanted my husband at home like other Amish fathers and husbands. But it was not to be. Although evenings were the hardest times for me with missing my husband, it was equally hard during the day to take care of our children and manage all the chores. At least I didn't have to go milk at "Pep Wayne's" (what we—and all the Amish—called Johnny's brother). Our one cow was now in our own barn. But it took me between an hour and a half and two hours a day to milk, feed the hogs, and help the sows birth their baby pigs.

In the winter the children stayed inside while I chored, because it was too cold for them to be out with me. They sat on our library table right in front of the big picture window and watched me as I went from the barn to the hog house and all the other places I trekked while doing the chores. Michael, who was about seven, often beat on the window or yelled out the door every half hour or so, "When will you be done? Malinda is crying . . ." Then Mark or Elizabeth would beat on the window. And so it went.

"Just (so many) more minutes or (so many) more pigs," I'd say, trying to appease them. I would go on with my chores, trying to get them all completed quickly so that I could care for the children. I felt sorry I had to leave the children inside, but I also knew the chores had to be done; the animals had to be fed and cared for. As I went about, I could keep my eyes on the kids through the window. I pitied them standing there watching me, waiting for me to come back in. But payments had to be made, and Johnny had to have his other job to make ends meet. What else could I do?

One evening when Malinda was still a baby, I came into the basement after finishing my chores. We always entered through the basement after doing chores, so we could leave our dirty boots and muddy clothes there and clean up before going upstairs. I cleaned up and went up the stairs, but I found the door at the top of the stairway closed tight. I couldn't open it. My first thought was that Michael must have locked it some way, but then I remembered it didn't have a lock. So I pushed harder, and it seemed something was on the other side.

Shoving the door open, I found little Malinda lying on the floor, holding her empty bottle. She was sucking on air and had traces of tears on her cheeks. Even though she was asleep, her breath still came in little broken gasps from all the sobbing she done. She knew that this was the door I went out to do chores, and she had placed herself right there where I couldn't even open the door. I broke down and cried when I picked her up. I held poor little Malinda and felt sorry that I had to leave her there, crying so hard and so long, while I was outside doing chores.

During those two long years I prayed for strength to keep on keeping on. "One day at a time, sweet Jesus, that's all I'm asking of you," I sang many times to keep going and to keep my spirits up. Once everyone was fed, bathed, and tucked into bed, I was able to have some quiet time with my Lord. In that way I was renewed in my spirit, ready to face another day.

⸺

After we had been farming Wayne's place for three years, I started having misgivings about my abilities as an Amish wife and mother. This was in the summer of 1971. Johnny was still farming and working days at the window-and-door plant. We had six children, three in diapers, which was beginning to overwhelm me. My workload was at its peak in the middle of canning season. I was in a family way again, and getting run-down, physically and emotionally.

Because our two babies slept in their baby beds in our bedroom, I was constantly awake at night. Several times a night I had to get up to feed the babies, and, with feeding and changing, it was an hour or two each time until I could get back to bed and try to catch a little bit of sleep. Even though I sorely needed naps in the afternoons after being up each night for feedings, the children were always too loud for me to take them. Lack of sleep, along with the pressing weight of all the other duties that a good Amish wife should do, made me want to leave it all.

A consuming thought started going through my mind: *Just walk away . . . just walk away. You can't do it all. This is too much.* I still loved Johnny and my children, I still wanted to believe and keep the Amish faith, but I was terribly overwhelmed, and I continually allowed this thought to consume me: *I'm not good enough to be an Amish wife.*

The other Amish wives seemed to embody an ideal of industry and kindness I could never live up to. During this time an Amish relative called me "lazy," which hurt me deep down to the core. I had tried very hard to be a dedicated Amish wife and mother, had spent several years studying and learning this life, and I knew absolutely in my spirit that the Lord wanted me to be Amish. But I didn't know how I could go on any longer.

For about two weeks, the feelings of being overwhelmed just consumed me. Outside, I had sows and pigs to feed and a hundred chickens to tend to, in addition to collecting and washing the eggs. Inside, I had three babies in cloth diapers, which I had to wash—no Pampers for us. Then there was the continual cycle of washing, cleaning, sewing, baking, ironing—back then I ironed all our everyday clothes in addition to our church clothes—meals to make, children to bathe, and always dishes and dishes and dishes to wash.

Gardening, about which I knew little, what with my city upbringing, was the hardest chore for me. It seemed I could never keep up with the weeds. Then the canning for our ever-expanding family would begin. In the summer I canned many different kinds of fruits and vegetables. Even in the winter the canning continued, as we preserved the beef, hogs, and chickens that we raised and butchered. We put up hundreds upon hundreds of quarts of food each year. Many times I thought, *How in the world will I ever get this canning done?*

It's not that Johnny didn't help me when he could. But with farming morning and nights at our place and Wayne's, and working eight hours at the factory, he could only do so much. I still brag about how many dirty diapers Johnny rinsed out in the toilet and then rinsed in the sink before I washed them on washday. Sometimes when he came home at night, I had whole piles of dirty diapers waiting to be taken care of. Johnny would look at them and say, "I will do this." And he took them, rinsed each one in the toilet, rinsed it again in the sink, and hung it to dry either on the side of the bathtub or on the rinse tub in the basement. If we didn't hang them to dry, those diapers would mildew by washday.

Not only were the diapers piling up, my feelings of being overwhelmed were piling up, too. It wasn't that I wanted to quit being Amish or leave Johnny, but I just couldn't cope any longer. I began thinking, *My mom was right. I can't handle this life anymore.*

⊕━━━━━━━━━⊕

One gloomy day with overcast skies, my mood as glum as the weather, I sat down and wrote Johnny a note. I told him that I really loved him and the children, but that I couldn't go on any longer with the overwhelming responsibilities. I just had to leave. I even said I would wear my Amish clothes and believe my Amish faith, but mentally I couldn't take my life any longer.

I had my leaving all planned. I thought, *When Johnny goes to work, I'll ask Lizzie or someone to babysit. Then I'll walk to Beach City, so he doesn't know where I am. He'll never think I would go back home knowing how bad things are between my mom and me.*

I sat in the kitchen and wrote my note, heaviness and despair hanging over me. Stuffing it in an envelope, I wrote "To Johnny" on the outside and stood there, staring at the words. With tears welling up, I took the note into the bedroom to place on our dresser.

As I propped up the note so he would see it, tears streaming down my face onto my dress, something or Someone prompted me inside, saying, "You cannot do this. Remember how much you have always loved him. You *cannot* do this." Kneeling down, I began to pray beside our bed. I prayed and cried for at least a half hour, sobbing my heart out to God.

Finally the tears subsided, and I asked God, "Help me to do the right thing . . . to quit thinking so much of what I'm going to do." My broken thoughts were jumbled as I struggled with my decision. "Let me do the right thing in your eyes. I know I love Johnny . . . I just can't see how I can do this. Am I being selfish? Just help me. I need your arms around me. . . . Just please help me."

Suddenly, at that moment, the sun came out, streaming through the window on the left, the beams shining right on me, over my back and onto my left shoulder. The brightness and warmth of that light transfixed me. I brought my head up to the bright sun, and I knew it was the touch of the Lord. I felt him so strongly. His comforting presence just wrapped around me, and I think he was crying with me and for me. It was such a riveting experience—I will never forget it.

I basked in the light as my bedroom was filled with peace and joy and God's glory. All in an instant the despair and anguish left me. It lifted right off, and I thought, *This is like the day God took those weights off me when I was saved.*

I looked up and said, "Thank you, Lord. I won't go." I walked out of our bedroom with my note, tore it up, and threw it away.

Immediately my thoughts changed. *Life will get better. Love does amazing things. Marlene, you can endure. Get up . . . things will get better.* I went out and took up my duties with a renewed heart and mind. I felt good, and I was fine. I never again felt despair to that extent, and never again wanted to walk away from it all.

Yes, I still had times of frustrations, times I needed a break. Years later, I was once more weighed down with all the responsibilities facing me. Seeing my state, Johnny said after dinner, "I'll take care of the dishes and the kids. You just take a few minutes. Go for a walk by yourself."

I walked out to our pond, my eyes floating over the empty waters, sat down at our picnic table, and poured my heart out to God. In weariness I put my head down and said, "Lord, will I make it? I know you hear me, but I need to hear your assurance." I asked God to do something special for me, and told God that I would just love to see a duck or a couple of swans on the pond.

I sat quietly for a moment. When I raised my head, I couldn't believe it. There was a duck! I blinked my eyes and even tilted my head to make sure I was seeing what I had asked for. Again,

just like the day many years earlier when I prayed at my bed-
side, God flooded my heart and gave me the assurance that he
would see me through.

I pray often that all of our children could find such peace,
and I pray for them the blessing in Numbers 6:24-26: "The
Lord bless thee, and keep thee: The Lord make his face shine
upon thee, and be gracious unto thee: The Lord lift up his
countenance upon thee, and give thee peace." God's words have
brought me much comfort throughout our marriage.

Johnny and I have discussed many times what might have
happened early on in our marriage if we hadn't accepted Jesus
as our Savior. I probably would have been like my mom: a bit-
ter, angry, jealous woman. Johnny says that we would have
divorced in fewer than five years. Thank you, Lord, for your
love, mercy, and grace. Walking in grace is the true meaning of
John's words in John 3:30: more of Christ, less of me.

Part III

14

Our Hundred-Acre Farm

AFTER HAVING ONE child at the hospital and five home births, I thought it was time to go to "Bill Barb's" for this delivery to get some rest. Bill and Barb Hostetler were an Amish couple who opened their home to Amish women for their deliveries. (The Amish have their own way of identifying people, which gives a kind of genealogy or reference. Often when referring to a married couple, we link the first names together. In this case, Bill and Barb became "Bill Barb's.")

After I had Wayne, the doctor had given me some bad news. "Marlene, I think you should consider not having any more children because your hernia is very bad. Having more babies will only make it worse." I thought, *I'll make it all right; I only have six children.* I didn't even imagine then that I'd have four more. Barb was like a midwife, and she had learned her trade through hands-on training. She opened her home to Amish women to come and stay during their labors, and she helped deliver the babies, for which she charged a small fee. Barb didn't have a set price, just a sliding-scale fee, asking people to pay what they could afford. The two times I went to Bill Barb's, we asked her what most people were paying and paid her that amount. She didn't do this wonderful service for money; she just had a gift and loved serving women in this way. She even delivered lots of her own grandchildren and great-grandchildren.

Two doctors from the Mount Eaton Clinic, Dr. Eberly and Dr. Lehman, came to deliver babies at Bill Barb's. Later some of the doctors got together and decided to build a birthing center for the Amish in Mount Eaton, because Barb was getting old and had to have one or two hired girls all the time. When I went to Bill Barb's in 1971 and 1973 for two of my deliveries, she only had a hired girl on Monday to do her washing. Barb did everything else for her home and the women in labor herself. She made nutritious meals three times a day and washed, ironed, cleaned, and gardened. Barb and her husband were so gracious to open their home to complete strangers and to care for new mothers and their children. If the mother didn't nurse, Barb and Bill took care of the baby at night to give the mother rest. Many nights, I could hear Barb moving about caring for the mothers and babies. Often she must have had hardly any sleep.

Barb and Bill have since passed away, but I feel they are surrounded by hundreds of little children in heaven. Besides Johnny's mom and my grandma, Bill and Barb were two of the most saintly people I knew. If they didn't get their reward in heaven, I don't know who would.

This baby was due in December 1971, right around Christmas. Each year Johnny and I took a day to go Christmas shopping at Dover. That was the one day out of the year that we hired someone to babysit, so that we could be together to buy our family presents. This year we went Christmas shopping a little early, as I knew I would soon be going to Bill Barb's. I wanted to have all the presents wrapped and ready for our family before the baby came.

I started in labor on the evening of December 23, and we hired a driver to take us to Bill Barb's. Barb checked me when I got there, and said things weren't going very fast. After I was there for a while, the labor stopped.

When the doctor came the next day, he said, "Marlene, your labor is not progressing very quickly. If you don't want to go home tonight without a baby, you can come to my office and I'll put an IV drip in you to help speed things along."

Well, I didn't want to go home without my baby, so I went with him to his office. He put me in one of his examination rooms and hooked me up to an IV. I stayed in that one little room hooked up to the IV all day and into the evening before my labor was hard enough to be able to go back to Barb's for the delivery.

The day stretched out, as my labor went on and on with nothing for me to do. For a while I lay on the table and tried to relax. Then I walked to the window and watched people going to the bank across the street. I watched people come into the clinic and later saw them leave in their cars. Amish people came in with buggies, hitched up to the post, and went to the bank or the clinic. When I grew tired of looking out the window, I read for a while. The labor went on and on.

Around seven in the evening, after the doctor's office hours were over, Dr. Eberly's wife brought his meal and something for me to eat, too. I hadn't eaten anything all day, following Barb's usual advice during labor. When the doctor came in to my room with the plateful of food, he said, "I want you to eat this."

I looked at the food and my mouth began to water. "Barb told me not to eat," I said.

"Well, *I* told you to eat," he said. "I want you to have some strength for this delivery." So I dug in, happy to have nourishment and strength for the rest of my labor and delivery.

Later that evening, December 24, 1971, we were finally blessed with our baby—our biggest one yet, at seven pounds and fifteen ounces. We named our boy Stephen after Stephen in the Bible, who was stoned to death for his faith.

Our Stephen had a round face, blond hair, blue eyes, and lots of fuzz all over his face. He looked just like a peach. When he was older, I wished he had also acted like a peach. He was so naughty. My sister-in-law Barbara called him a blister, because he was kind of like a blister or thorn in your flesh. He'd do something naughty, and then he'd just smile at you and laugh. So, my sister-in-law would say, "He's a little blister." It seemed Stephen was always sneaking something to put into his pockets. He got many a spanking for his stealing and sneaking, but it didn't help. He just kept on, through his adolescent years.

The night that he was born, however, Stephen was our little peach, full of promise. After his birth I stayed three days at Bill Barb's, enjoying their loving care and taking time to rest. Since it was Christmastime, Johnny was able to stay home to take care of our other children. He didn't have to work, because the plant always shut down between Christmas and New Year's. We were happy he could be home to help because we did not feel it was right to take a hired girl from her family at Christmas.

Johnny told the children they could open their presents when I got home with the new baby. During those days he was home with the children, Johnny took time to play games with them and read a lot. Reading is still one of his favorite pastimes. No one starved during those days I was gone, but I'm sure Johnny made plenty of hot dogs and eggs-in-the-hole for supper. There was probably cereal for breakfast, lunchmeat sandwiches for lunch, and lots and lots of my canned apple-sauce and fruit.

A couple of days after Christmas, I came home with Stephen. As soon as I got home, our eager children got to open their gifts, and our hired girl came to help. We had a wonderful Christmas that year, praising the Lord for his great gifts to us: our perfect child, our family, and our Savior, Jesus Christ.

Just before Stephen's birth, in the fall, we bought a farm one mile away from where we were living. Because it was close by, we could still be in the same church district, which is what we desired. The English man who owned it had over one hundred head of sheep and raised elderberries that he sold to a jam-and-jelly company. After the company said he had to get some very expensive equipment for the elderberries, he decided to sell. Johnny went to look at the farm first and thought there might be some potential for us to live and farm there. Then I went and looked, too. I liked the location and the land, but the house looked awful. I always called it the "cracker-box house" because it was so little.

"A family of nine could not live in this little house! No way," I told Johnny when we went to see it.

But Johnny said, "If we buy this place, we'll borrow enough to add on and fix it up."

The seller decided he wanted to sell "lock, stock, and barrel," as the English saying goes. He just wanted to walk away from all of it.

Buildings on the hundred-acre farm before Johnny and Marlene bought it in 1971. The barn was yellow then. They began remodeling the house and moved into it in March 1972.

With thankful hearts and hope for the future, we bought our hundred-acre farm, along with all the farm equipment and the sheep. It seemed like our prayers were answered. We needed a bigger farm so Johnny wouldn't have to work away from home. He really wanted to farm full time, and we wanted him home with us more than anything.

Because the house was too small for our family, we stayed put in our current house until we could remodel and move. Each day after he got home from his job at four o'clock in the afternoon, Johnny worked in the fields at our new farm. He had to bulldoze all the hilled-up elderberries and sow wheat in the fall, so we would have a crop come summer. Plus he had to feed the sheep every day until we sold them.

One evening after work, Johnny was in a hurry to hitch our buggy horse onto the hack and get to the new farm. This horse had been newly shod just a day or two before, with sharp edges to his shiny new shoes. I was standing there, taking advantage of a few precious minutes to talk to Johnny before he was gone again. As often happened, young Mark was underfoot. "Can I go?" he pleaded. "Can I go with you, Daddy?"

"No, I'm in a hurry."

Mark was about four years old then, and he loved being with his daddy and being around the horses.

While Johnny was busy with the hitching, Mark got too close to the horse. Johnny swung that horse around to back him into the hack, and the horse stepped right on Mark's foot, turning on it and grinding it into the gravel. Mark began screaming. I stood there watching the entire scene unfold as if in slow motion, watching the horse swing around, seeing Mark back there, his foot under the horse's shoe, and blood spreading over the gravel stones. I grabbed Mark and rushed him to our back porch. Blood was streaming from his foot.

I put his foot in a pan of cold water, trying to wash away enough blood to see the extent of the damage. I kept dumping and filling the water, dumping and filling the water, but the blood just kept running. I think I dumped the water away six times before we could see that his middle toe was mashed and dangling, but still hanging on.

Being Amish, we had learned to deal with most mishaps and emergencies ourselves, but this was one time we called the doctor. We asked him to come to the office that evening to check out Mark's toe, and it was pretty bad. He had to have many stitches, both inside and out, plus medication to protect against possible infection from all the gravel ground into his foot. After the driver brought Johnny and Mark back home, Johnny still had to go down to our big farm and feed the sheep. That was one night he was out very late doing the chores.

There was never a dull moment from the first child on. Not only were there lots of accidents, but there were always those mountains of diapers to wash. After I was married, I had learned to wash with a wringer-washer at the Ashery. The owners had a wringer-washing machine and offered to let me use it, which I was happy to do. Then I didn't have to go to the laundromat, which saved us money. So I learned to wash in the boiler room of the Ashery, where there was a steam hose we used to heat the water. That was new for me! I didn't know anything about steam, but I knew I could get badly burned if I got any on me. So I listened closely to directions and followed them carefully. Although I never got burned with the steam, I did get shocked more than once. I couldn't figure out why, but when I reached into the water I often got shocked. Of course, there was almost always water on the floor, too, which didn't help.

After being shocked several times, I told Johnny, "I will go to the laundromat if this continues. Would you take a look at the cord on the washer? I can see the wires." I wondered if that could be the problem, because the cord was frayed from many years of use. Johnny taped up the cord, and I was not shocked after that.

After becoming Amish, I didn't have steam available for my wash water. I used a kerosene hot water heater at our first farm. Using kerosene to heat the water was fantastic—very easy and not so scary to use—but the gasoline motor on the washing machine was a challenge. It surely tested my patience. Pulling the rope almost tore my insides out, or so I felt. Thankfully, for some years now I have had an air motor on my washing machine. I just push a little lever and it starts. Of course, it only starts this way if the diesel has run and created enough air pressure in the big pressure tanks outside. It takes a lot of pressure to wash for a couple of hours.

Even as our family grew, I only washed once or twice a week. Sometimes it took me from eight o'clock in the morning until at least noon, because our family created a lot of wash, especially diapers. For every new baby, I bought another four or five dozen diapers. The boys were very hard to potty train—mostly they were in diapers until age three or older—but the girls were potty trained at two. On washday, along with all of our clothes, I washed many dozens of diapers and many receiving blankets, which I used on the toddlers for night diapers. Oh yes, with ten children born in thirteen years, we had years and years of lots of diapers.

In the winter of 1971–72, Johnny and his brother Wayne poured a footer to build on to the little cracker-box house at our new farm. To save money, Johnny bulldozed the basement part himself. He did this in the evening after coming home from work, often working in the dark, thankful for any moonlight that helped him to see. Then he and Wayne laid blocks for the foundation, which was a muddy business. They ended up laying the blocks in mud and water, not only because it rained often but also because there was a spring in the back part of the old house.

In the basement of the existing part of the house was a small room with cement walls and floor where the spring water ran through a couple of cement troughs. There was a deep trough for pumping water to the upstairs, and a small trough where I placed our milk jars to keep them cold in the constantly running water. We did away with our icebox once we moved to our new farm, because we thought we could keep everything cold in this spring water pantry, especially in the winter. We used that room as a cooler for twenty-two years, occasionally buying bags of ice for special events.

When Johnny came home in the middle of summer, he was so very hot from working outside all day loading semis with windows and doors. He usually lay on the cold floor in our spring water pantry for about ten minutes to cool down before he came upstairs. This was very refreshing to him and a great respite from our hot and muggy summers.

As wonderful as that spring was as a cooler, it didn't come without its hazards. Accidents occurred there several times. A few years and several children later, while I was in the basement kitchen, I heard a sound like someone gurgling in water. It came again and again. Finally, I realized what that sound was—someone was in the water trough! I had baby Esther in my arms as I ran back to the spring room, where I saw little Stephen upside down in the deep water trough. He was submerged in the water with his head on the bottom and his legs up in the air. I reached down, grabbed him by his suspenders, and pulled him out of the water. Laying Esther on the couch in the basement, I took Stephen out on the lawn to resuscitate him. He hadn't turned blue yet, and soon he began coughing and throwing up.

I told the older kids, "Run down and tell your dad that Stephen fell in the water trough."

Johnny came up from the field and took one look at Stephen, who was now breathing. "Well, if he would listen, this wouldn't have happened." He had told the children many times to be careful in the spring room and to stay out of that trough. Stephen had gone in there because he was thirsty and was trying to get a drink of the nice, cold spring water flowing through our trough. This water was tempting to our children, because it was free-flowing and easy for them to reach.

After that accident, we put a board across the trough so none of the children could fall in. But even with that precaution, we had another incident four years later. Again, I was in my basement kitchen when I heard two crazy noises. Then it dawned on me: the noises were coming from the water trough. I ran back and there was Esther, flipped over on her back on the board, yelling as loud as she could with water from the water pipe running in and out of her mouth. As she was trying to get a drink, she placed her left hand on the board to steady herself. When she reached in with a glass in her right hand, her left hand slipped on the board, because it was damp and slippery, and she flipped over, getting stuck in an awkward position that she couldn't get out of. The water pipe was level with her mouth, and she was trying to yell while the water streamed in her mouth. I pulled her out, thankful that I had been close enough to hear her gurgles and rescue her.

⸺⸺⸺⸺

The first time we remodeled, we completely turned the floor plan around. The tiny bedroom became our pantry and part of the kitchen. The living room also became part of the kitchen, which was enlarged even more as we added an extension to it.

The kitchen, which had a stairway, became our bedroom, and a tiny one at that. The front door of the cracker-box house became our bedroom door, and we finished our remodel of the upstairs with the addition to the kitchen and by adding a large living room. We then added steps to the cellar off the kitchen, because the steps were originally outside. Johnny's nephews, Harry's Ivan and Wayne, helped him to tear the old porch off to start remodeling.

When it came time to choose colors for our new kitchen, I decided I wanted a color other than pink. I liked pink and had pink in every house from the time I was a little girl. After I moved out of my baby bed when I was about six or seven, Grandma Smith fixed up my bedroom. She paid to have the wallpaper hung and she also paid for the pink linoleum. My bedspread and pillowcases were pink, and the wallpaper had pink flowers. After I got married, I had more pink in our trailer with a pink sink, stove, and fridge, and even a pink sink and bathtub in the bathroom. When we moved into our first farmhouse, the kitchen and the bathroom were painted pink. I liked pink, but boy, after a while it gets to you! I was finally "pinked out," and for this new kitchen I was ready for a different color. I wanted yellow countertops this time. Yellow seemed cheery and modern. That's when I found out that looking at a little piece of Formica and suddenly seeing many feet of Formica are two different things.

When Johnny was putting in our countertops, he came home and said, "Wait until you see your countertops." He must have had some idea of how I would react. When they were done, I went over to see them. I almost fell backward when I saw our new countertops shining in the sunlight. They were bright yellow. *Really* bright and *really* yellow. I hadn't wanted any squiggly accents or patterns in them, so these were plain yellow, and really, really bright.

Johnny took one look at my astonished face and said, "Whenever I can afford it, we'll get other ones someday." I never did get those other ones until our children were grown and I moved into the doddy house. (The doddy house, or *Dawdy Haus*, is a small house for grandparents nearby or connected to the house of one of their adult children.) When we went to pick out our countertops for our doddy house, Johnny said, "Please don't get bright yellow ones."

He picked out a neutral beige color that looked nice, and I thought, *I'd better listen to him this time. Obviously I'm not good at picking out countertop colors.* So we ordered his choice, and I really liked it.

Not willing to let this issue rest, when Johnny picked out the shingles for the roof, he said, "I'm going to pick out the shingle color, too. I'm not going to let you ruin that." Maybe he was a little afraid of having a color that would be an embarrassment, shining out to the whole neighborhood for years. His choice prevailed, and I have to say they really look nice.

Dear Lizzie, who never seemed to tire of helping us, did all the sanding and varnishing of the woodwork for our remodel. Lizzie told me, "You can't go over to your new house with all your kids and expose them to those smells. I'll go over and do it." Most of the time I couldn't help with the remodeling because of caring for our seven children. I had all I could manage doing all the cooking, cleaning, laundry, and gardening for our family, along with caring for our hogs, chickens, and cow.

We tried, whenever we could, to sit down together as a family for meals, but often this wasn't possible when Johnny was working away from home and remodeling our farmhouse. One evening I harnessed the horse to the buggy myself and took supper to Johnny to surprise him. I must say he was really surprised. I had watched Johnny harness our horse many times, and, as usual, I had asked many questions because of my strong desire to learn.

Whenever Johnny was home, especially when he was farming or doing chores, I tried to be with him, watching him work and helping. It seemed he liked having me and the children beside him, even though I asked many questions. He had a lot of patience with me, answering my questions and explaining what he was doing. The children loved him dearly, and they loved those times of being with their daddy, too.

15

Moving to the Farm, Hosting Church

IN MARCH 1972, after nearly nine years of marriage, we moved with teams of horses and wagons to our newly remodeled house on our hundred-acre farm. Some neighbors and some of Johnny's relatives helped.

I never bothered to ask my family. When my mom saw our house before we remodeled it, she said, "I'll burn it down so you don't have to move there." Once the remodeling was done she seemed to have changed her opinion, because then she brought neighbors and friends to see it.

We made the move in only one day. There were lots of boxes left to unpack over the next few days, but we were moved in. Lizzie and I made food for the moving crew. The Amish have great organization for moving. The men make sure to put all the beds up first thing. Then the women make the beds, put up curtains, and put away as many staples as they can. They make sure the basics are ready so that a family can function. That was how it worked when we moved. Two weeks later, we had a sale for the equipment and sheep that came with the farm. We put the money from that sale toward our remodeling.

At the time of the move, Michael was eight and in third grade and Elizabeth was six and in first grade. Michael already knew how to milk a little, because we had the one cow on our twelve-acre place. For a couple of years, until some of the other children got old enough, he was the only one of the kids milking. The girls needed to be a little older for their hands to be strong enough. When the girls did start milking, we put two girls on each cow until the girls got old enough to milk a cow by themselves. Normally a person milks sitting on the right side of the cow, but we trained our cows to be milked with a girl on each side. The boys always had their own cow to milk.

We also brought our hog house along to our new place, as we had built it on skids in case we should move. It seemed there were always sows getting pigs. Each day, I went out to make sure the process went smoothly. The sows getting ready to deliver lay down in the pens Johnny had made for them. I reached in over the high railing, grabbed the baby pig after it was delivered, and wiped off its nose and mouth with a cloth. Then I placed it where it could suckle the sow right away, especially in the winter. Those baby pigs needed some nice, warm milk soon after birth to warm them up, or they might freeze to death. Then I reached down, grabbed the next pig, and started the process all over.

These daily chores became automatic to me, just part of life. Most of the time I never really thought about what I was doing. If I had time to think, it was, *I wasn't going to marry a stinkin' farmer, and here I am one! I must be crazy!* Or: *I can't believe I'm doing this. My mom would drop over dead if she saw me now!*

Once when I told my mom about chopping off a chicken's head, she said, "Are you *nuts*?"

"No," I said. "Why would I be nuts?"

"I'd never eat the chicken if I chopped its head off."

I said, "Mom, you've never been hungry enough." It was a mystery to me how she thought chickens got to the store. I know she would have just fallen over if she had seen me out there watching baby pigs being born and wiping off their faces.

It wasn't that I had it so bad, but it was a big transition to this life from the one I had growing up. Later, telling my daughter-in-law about the gift I got one year for Christmas, I had to laugh.

"What do you want for Christmas this year? I'll buy you whatever you want," Johnny offered.

"A pair of insulated boots," I said. "My toes are freezing outside when I chore."

So he went to the harness shop and got me some boots with liners. I was very happy when I unwrapped my new boots, and I was happy all the rest of the winter with my gift. No longer was I out in the freezing cold of winter, knocking my feet together to try to keep some blood flowing.

Hearing this story years later, my daughter-in-law said, "It's so funny you wanted to be a farmer. It's hard to imagine that you came from living in town and chose this life."

I said, "I wanted all kinds of animals. I just love animals." Heavy as the workload seemed to be at times, I loved being around the animals. I still do.

Then, too, I remembered I was the one who had chosen this. I had chosen Johnny, and I had chosen this life. We would never have become farmers if I hadn't pushed Johnny to do what I knew he loved. Right away when we got our first pigs at the Ashery, I knew he was born to be a farmer. Seeing him working with those pigs, I thought, *This is Johnny. He's a farmer.* I could just see it.

As our children came along, we knew that not only had Johnny and I to be willing to farm, the whole family needed to choose this life. It would take all of us pulling together to make it work. When we were on our twelve-acre farm and Johnny was working the afternoon shift, we'd kneel down to say our prayers each night before I'd put our three little children to bed. "Do we really want to farm? Do we want to pray for a big farm?" I'd often ask them.

"Oh, yeah," Michael and Elizabeth would eagerly say. Even little Mark would chime in his agreement: "Yeah." Every night we knelt, asking protection for Johnny at work and praying, "God, if you want us to have a bigger farm, open up the door, so Daddy can stay at home and not have to work away from here."

We made this decision as a family. We all agreed. At their young ages, the children may not have known all that this decision would entail for them in the future, but they knew they wanted to have their daddy at home. That's what they knew.

When we were on the big farm, I saw the benefits of farming. I could get out of the house, go to the barn where we milked, and be with Johnny. That got me away from the crying baby and the endless chores inside. Now I see young women, who are not on farms, constantly inside the house with their children, especially in the winter when they are not gardening. These young women often have more problems mentally and with depression than women who live on farms. The women on farms go outside and help their husbands in the fields, like I did. It can be a relief to get out of the house to do something different and be with your husband. You know what? After the hot, physical work in the field, I was glad to go back into the house to prepare a meal. When I was getting out of depression, God gave me strength, but farming also helped. It got me out of the house, and I got to be with the animals, which I loved. And many days, it was mind over matter. I just got up and went on.

When Michael was eight or nine, one of his cousins and some other boys in his grade started teasing him relentlessly. I don't know what the teasing was about—whether it was because his mother used to be English, or because we didn't have as much money as others, or something else. It could have been about shoes, because we couldn't afford more than one pair of school shoes for each child, and sometimes those were pretty worn. Whatever the cause, the teasing just wouldn't stop. A child can only take so much until he explodes. Many an afternoon Michael cried to me after school, and my heart ached for him. But I knew this was a situation that Michael had to handle himself. "I can't be there to fight your battles in life," I told him, "so you'll have to take care of this yourself and do whatever you have to do to survive."

I couldn't believe what he did! The next time those boys ganged up on him, he found a board, slammed the first boy in the head, and knocked him silly. That was the end of the bullying. From that time on they knew he meant business. I hadn't told him to do what he did, but I guess that's what it took for him to earn respect from those boys. I probably should have told him to turn the other cheek. But I believe we walk a fine line sometimes when teaching our children how to handle difficult situations. I didn't want to make him a target or have him hate school. In typical boyhood fashion, those boys became Michael's friends after that. In fact, they became true and faithful friends.

As I said before, Michael was afraid of the dark, but he loved the water. When he saw the former strip mine hole filled with water on the hill above our house, he begged to go swimming. With an old lifejacket and cut-off Amish pants, away he went. He learned to swim in that pond and so did all the other children. Michael claimed he taught all the other kids to swim, but Johnny helped them learn, too.

Often I let them go swimming for about two hours in the afternoon, after canning was done. Michael couldn't get enough swimming to suit him, and he and some of our other boys took big sandstones and a big board, and made a diving board. What fun they had!

After our farm sale, Johnny decided it was time to remodel our barn. He hired three and sometimes four Swartzentruber Amish boys to live with us during that time so the labor wouldn't cost too much. They lived with us for weeks until it was done. We installed a new milk house, cow stanchions, and horse stalls. We also made new barn doors to allow Johnny to drive straight through the barn with a manure spreader. Johnny's dad came almost every day to see that things were done right and to oversee the cementing. He taught the crew how to split sandstones the right way to use them as filler so we didn't need as much cement, which saved us quite a bit of money.

When the barn was finished, I must say it was a relief. All I did during those weeks of building was wash, bake, clean, and make meals. With all those extra hungry mouths to feed, as soon as one meal was done, it was time to start the next. Sometimes I used to think I'd go crazy with all the work and responsibilities. But I never had time!

That year, 1972, Johnny's dad had a hernia operation and was later diagnosed with cancer. He died that fall at age seventy-five. His death was a terrible blow for us, as everyone thought he would live to be a hundred. We all thought he was so healthy. I dearly loved him, and our hearts ached with his passing. Stephen was sick with an earache at that time, and I didn't think I'd be able to go to the funeral, but he was finally better by then. I was so glad to be there at the viewing. I knew we were going to miss Andy all the rest of our lives, and I wanted to be there to see him for the last time.

———

It was announced that church would be held at our place on the Sunday following the funeral. This would be the first time since we became Amish that we would have church. I didn't feel at all ready for having church, not only because of sick children and the funeral but because we weren't fully situated in our new home. But I thought, *If they want us to have church, we'll have church, mud and all.*

Having church at our place seemed a little overwhelming, and I wasn't even sure I knew what all it entailed. That was the hard part for me. People who grew up Amish knew how to get ready for church; they knew what weeks you washed all the walls, what weeks you washed all the bedding, what weeks you washed all the curtains. Spring cleaning was one thing, but getting ready for church entailed a whole lot more. Everyone who has church gets ready for it with an intense cleaning: washing walls, woodwork, curtains, and bedding; cleaning out closets, pantries, and storage areas; and washing ceilings and polishing furniture. Food must be prepared for lunch and dinner for all the people who come to church and those who can stay through the evening, and even for the women who come to help get ready. Many times I was up until midnight, stirring up cookies to get ready for the women coming to help the next day.

I didn't get all the drawers cleaned and arranged like some women do. To me it seemed like a losing battle to clean and organize the children's drawers. A person can get all the drawers arranged and then a child looks for some pants or something, and *whoosh*, there it goes—all your work is destroyed. There was still a big pile of soil and mud in our front yard, and most of our outside walls weren't washed off from the muddy winter construction. Having those things done seemed to me just the very basics of getting ready for church.

Johnny had to get a lot of things ready, too. He had to get all the manure out of the barn, clean the barn windows, clean the milk house, and wash the milk house windows. We did our very best, but without the help of Johnny's aunts, cousins, and our neighbors, we wouldn't have gotten ready.

Because it was fall, we had church in our home, but Johnny and I loved it during the summer when we had church in someone's barn. Fresh, clean hay was laid in the upper part of the barn where church was held, and it smelled so nice. It also helped to entertain the children, as they braided it and played with it. Now most of the Amish have shops where they have church. But to this day, we both still love it whenever we have church in a barn.

Later on, during hunting season, it was even more difficult for us to get ready when we had church. We had six boys, at least four of whom hunted with Johnny during any given year. And where do you think all their hunting equipment and gear would collect? The basement. All those coats, guns, shells, and boots were piled up on the table down there. Here we would be, trying to put everything away, to make everything spic-and-span, and to make room for tables in every spare corner and places to put all the food we were preparing for the hundreds of people. "We're trying to have church, and here's all this hunting gear," I reminded them. But it seemed there was no place to put all their gear. It was a big trial. But somehow, each year we made it work.

After church we fed everyone the usual lunch—peanut butter, luncheon meat, Swiss cheese, pickles, pickled red beets, pies, cookies, and coffee. The first year we had church, when it came time for everyone to go home, many of the boys helped people board their buggies. I'm sure there were some pretty muddy boys who left our place that afternoon.

It was an absolute relief to have it over. I was so happy my house was clean and there were plenty of cookies left. I couldn't help but think about how many muddy children went home that day. With some ordeals, I used to say, "If I can make it through this, I can make it through anything." Always the first time through anything is the worst: the first wedding, the first church, the first funeral. It was all new to me. I knew how other people got ready for things, but when I had to have the events at my place, it was a learning process for me.

I learned to press through and work until things were ready. If I had to work until midnight or later, I did it. If I had to sit with my feet up on a footstool for a while to rest them, I sat for fifteen minutes, then got back up and did what had to be done. The process was the same for church, for weddings, and even for Christmas Eve. I got so tired from baking and cleaning that when things were finally ready and people came, I often sat down and almost went to sleep.

On the night after we had church at our place for the first time, I sat down, put my feet up, and had some cookies. What a blessed relief!

16

The Bountiful Years

YOU HAVE TO have a love of farming or you will never do it. We did have that love of farming, and we worked hard for many years. We raised wheat, oats, corn, hay, and silage on our new farm. We started farming with four Belgian horses, and in later years we used six. Those Belgians were really tough, because they had so many hills to play "tug of war" on, as we used to say. Many other farmers said their horses couldn't pull as well as ours because most of their farms were level.

Now that we had a bigger place we enlarged our operation of raising hogs, but we downsized raising chickens for eggs because I had quit selling eggs. With our larger family, we only had enough eggs and chickens for ourselves. We did raise fifty broilers (male chickens that are sterilized). When it came time to butcher and can these broilers, Lizzie always came to help me, as it was an all-day job. Johnny chopped the heads off, and Lizzie and I had a big tub of hot water ready to plunge the chickens into so we could pull the feathers off. There were always tricks to every chore around the farm, including heating water for scalding the feathers off the chickens. It couldn't be too hot, or it would scald the skin on the chicken, but it couldn't be too lukewarm, or the feathers wouldn't pull out well. We boiled water in a large teakettle, which we replenished throughout the day. Later on I skinned my chickens, because I never did get the trick of getting the water just the right temperature. Lizzie was the expert on that.

We had a herd of ten Holstein cows, which we milked each morning and evening. Johnny's dad, Andy, had bought our first cow, and we bought another nine with the money from the farm sale. Eventually we had twenty-two. In those first years I milked three cows, Michael two, and Johnny the rest. Every morning the alarm went off at five o'clock, and up and at it Johnny would go. But first, before he headed out to the barn to feed the animals and get the milk buckets ready, he always knelt in prayer.

When the cows were all in the barn, Johnny got a small bucket with hot, soapy water and a rag to wash their udders. I couldn't stand any dirt or debris on our cows' udders, because it might fall into the milk bucket. We were especially careful since we sold milk either to the cheese factory for making Swiss cheese or to the dairy for milk. After milking each cow by hand, we carried the milk into the milk house. There we poured it through a strainer into eighty-pound milk cans to strain out any remaining dirt particles.

In the summer we kept the cows in our pasture close the barn so Johnny and our trusty dog, Rusty, didn't have to go far to find them and bring them into the barn for milking. Rusty was as good as a hired hand when it came time to find those cows and bring them in.

What all I learned during those years! And the learning was growing by leaps and bounds, now, with our increased acreage and increased crops.

The children made their own fun on the farm, and we got joy from watching their antics. We raised a bull as a pet and kept him in a bull pen Johnny had made. Johnny had also made a feeding trough in the alley where the cows came out of the barn, and this bull knew how to twist his head out through the bars. He had little stubby horns that the kids took hold of, trying to shake his head. The bull seemed to love it. "How are you doing, Bully?" they would ask, and then they would pet his head.

One day one of the children said, "I'm going to sit on his head," and he did. He sat on the bull's head while it bobbed up and down. Seeing the fun and not to be outdone, the next boy said, "I'm going to try it, too!" Then another one did it. It was usually the boys who did this risky activity, which quickly became a new game with them. They thought it was kind of like teeter-totter. When people saw our children riding the bull while he bobbed them up and down, they just laughed and laughed. They couldn't believe our bull would give them rides like that. It was so funny to all of us.

Milking went on year-round, but early in the spring we started plowing with our Belgian horses. Most often Johnny used a walking plow—a plow pulled by a team of horses as the farmer walks behind. Other times he used a riding plow— one he could sit on, but which was still pulled by our Belgians. The walking plow is not as big as a riding plow, and it just makes one furrow.

I never knew anyone who could plow as well as Johnny. I tried it once, and went about six or eight feet. The horses took off, and then *whoop*, there went the plow onto its side in the field. I couldn't push the plow down hard enough to keep it in the ground. I learned right then that it takes a lot of strength to push a plow. After trying some of these things, I gained a lot of respect for farmers who would walk behind their plows for hours and hours, miles and miles, to prepare the fields for planting and sowing.

I didn't know anything about farming, but Johnny sure did, and I worked alongside him as much as I could, learning as I went along. We—or shall I say *he*—sowed oats in the spring and harvested the hay several times a year, which was all brought loose into the barn. He never baled it until some years later. Big grab hooks on a pulley drawn by horses raised it off the hay wagon and loaded it into the barn. It was my job to drive the horses to pull the rope that raised the hay into the air. Once the hay was in the air, I pulled on a trip rope that made the grab hooks let loose. This dropped the hay into the hay mow in the barn attic . . . if all went well. Sometimes I almost got pulled up in the air if I didn't let go in time. Had I kept hanging on when this happened, I could easily have been slammed into the wagon.

One time I tripped a rope too quickly and the hay fell partly into the mow and partly back into the wagon. Sometimes I laughed at my struggles, but for the most part I got upset with myself. It's a wonder that Johnny didn't disown me at times, I felt so inept.

After the first hay cutting it was time to cut, shock, and thresh wheat. The grain is cut just before it is fully ripe, and then a grain binder, pulled by three or four horses, makes the sheaves. The grain binder was one of the largest pieces of machinery we had until we got balers. The sheaves came out of the binder tied with twine. When the kids were little we put the horses to rest, and then we all started to shock together. When our kids were old enough they could form the sheaves into shocks. This was a big job, and sometimes we gave the kids some incentives to work. "If you get this job done quickly, we'll buy you something," we'd tell them.

When I first saw shocks standing in the field, I thought those sheaves looked like little huts. To shock the wheat you stack the sheaf bundles with three in the middle, two on either side, and then you make a cap with another sheaf to keep the grain dry. Then you have to bend the cap down right, trying to keep all the grain protected. How many times did I hear, "Uh-oh! You have the butt end the wrong direction, Marlene. You have to have that facing out."

I learned to shock, but Johnny made most of the caps. To make a cap I took a sheaf under my arm, pressing a third of it down and to the right. Then I grabbed it with my other arm and pulled the other side down, and lastly I pulled the middle part downward. No matter how hard I tried, the caps I made always seemed to blow off in the first wind. I tried to do whatever I could to help on the farm, tried to do my part, even though my work was not always the best. Like I said before—it took a lot of patience to teach me to be an Amish farmer.

<hr />

After the wheat was shocked, it was time to thresh oats. The children got very excited when the threshing machine arrived with Uncle Wayne in command. They loved to watch Uncle Wayne handle that big thresher. And of course they helped however they could. When they were little they hauled water to the men in the fields, making sure they had plenty to drink.

When they got older they helped in the grain bin. Pep Wayne and Johnny's dad had been threshing with the big Huber tractor since Wayne was a teenager. Wayne sure knew his stuff with that tractor. I was fascinated by it too, and I watched those men thresh whenever I could.

Usually, however, I was too busy cooking to watch. When the threshing team arrives, the Amish wife has her day cut out for her. There were usually around ten to twelve extra men and boys bringing their teams and wagons with them—and bringing big appetites to the table after their day of hard work. My meal for these helpers consisted of fried chicken or meatloaf, mashed potatoes and gravy, Amish dressing, cold tossed salad or coleslaw, applesauce for my little ones, fruit, and Jell-O. For dessert I made tapioca pudding, date pudding, or a graham cracker pudding, with various cakes and pies. I'd sure be tired and full, just like the men, when these long harvest days ended.

If the men came to our farm after they had threshed another place where they had dinner, I only had to serve drinks, ice cream, and cake. On those days I could watch them in the fields. I was and still am in awe of Amish farmers who do things the old way. There was so much technique and finesse to what those farmers did. It's an art—very time consuming and labor intensive, but worth the effort for the results. I'm sad that it has become almost a lost art here in our church. We don't have too many farmers any more.

Threshing, in our opinion, kept the neighbors and the neighborhood in close contact, with everybody looking out for each other and helping each other. Isn't that what the Bible tells us to do? Part of the song we sang in our Girls' Ensemble says, "No man is an island, no man stands alone." How well that is practiced among the Amish! We are so privileged to have all these things passed down to us, all these traditions and practices shown to us.

If we had lots of rainfall during the growing season, we could expect a second and sometimes a third crop of hay. A farmer is always at the mercy of God for the weather and the crops. Thanks be to God that He is in control of the weather. If the majority of the population was in control, we'd have sun all summer with no rain. Before I became a farmer's wife I remember thinking like that—wanting sunshine all summer long.

Next on the list of crops was harvesting silage corn to fill the silo. Silage is what we fed the cows in the winter. It's very good feed for cows because it helps to keep their protein up. Every evening throughout the winter, while the cows were in the barn, Michael or one of the older boys would climb up the silo and throw pitchforkfuls of silage down into the chute. Johnny or I would shovel the silage from the bottom of this chute to feed the cows.

Again, neighbor men came with wagons and teams of horses to help harvest. Johnny cut all the corn stalks down with a corn binder the day before the men were to come. The corn binder cut the corn standing straight up, tied it up, and then kicked it out the back. Afterward, our whole field was covered with these corn stalks. Unlike hay or wheat or oats, silage corn does not need to be dry when harvested. A little rain is actually good for silage, but if it rained we hoped it wouldn't be too muddy for the men to get their wagons in and out of the field.

Last but not least on our yearly calendar of farm chores was the enormous job of husking the field corn by hand. We put this field corn in cribs to dry out and make feed for hogs and cows. When Johnny came home from an eight-hour shift at his job, we had a team of horses ready, and then we all headed to the field to make the rounds. During the three to four weeks it took to pick the corn by hand, Saturdays always found us out in the cornfield.

After Johnny's mother died he got her hand corn-husker. It kind of reminds me of half a glove—just the palm part with no fingers. There is a leather band that you place on your right hand with a strap. Attached to this band on the palm of the hand is a metal plate with a pick on it. We grabbed the ear of corn with the left hand, took the hand picker, and "whooshed" it to tear open the husk. Then we slipped our hand down over the ear to break it off with the rest of the husk still attached to the corn stalk. If we couldn't snap that ear of corn off, as happened sometimes for me, it was frustrating. Then we threw that ear onto a hay wagon with sides. Husking this way took quite a bit of hand strength, and often my wrists hurt during those weeks working in the cornfields.

But there was a rhythm to our work, especially the way Johnny did it: *Pick, grab, pitch. Pick, grab, pitch.* He did it so fast it wasn't even funny. It was an absolute art. Husking by hand left the fields clean and neat, not like the corn huskers they use now, which leave corn husks and corn stalks all over the field and all over the corn. Doing things the old way made farming an art, and I marveled at it.

I never could husk as fast as Johnny, but I sure gave it my best try. I had a hesitation in my rhythm: pulling the stalk down, husking, tearing the ear off, then finally pitching it on the wagon. For a town girl to learn to do this, there's got to be a will and a love for the great country air and the farm way of life.

I had all of those things. Like they say, "If there's a will, there's a way," and I certainly had the will to learn.

Even though it was hard work, I loved working alongside Johnny, being in the fields, and accomplishing these great tasks. It was good family time, too, with our older children beside us.

In the evening when we were done making hay, the children would put an old couch cushion on the hay rope. They found this cushion when we moved to our big farm, and they loved to sit on it and swing in the barn, yelling and laughing. Because it was such a long rope, they could swing as high as the peak in the barn. In my memories, I can still hear them laugh and laugh. Johnny held the little ones and swung, too. With any leisure time Johnny had, he was always playing with the children.

As these harvesting times drew to a finish, it was a wonderful and blessed feeling to have the barn and the silo filled to the brim. But we never really had time to bask in contentment, because now the cows were in the barn and there was feeding to do every day and lots of manure to deal with. In the summer, there was much to be done in the fields; in the winter, there was much to be done in the barn.

The first summer on the farm, with ten acres of each crop, we got four small wagonloads of hay, thirty-five bushels of wheat per acre, fifty-five bushels of oats per acre, and one hundred bushels of corn per acre. It took about two and a half acres of silage corn to fill the silo, and the rest of our farmland was pasture for our animals. It took quite a few years to get the fields to produce at the level we desired, but by the time we retired from farming in 1995, the difference was really noticeable. In

186 · CALLED TO BE AMISH

the end, we had two hundred bushels of corn, fifty bushels of wheat, and eighty bushels of oats per acre.

Besides the crops, we had buggy horses, workhorses, chickens, cows, pigs, sheep, cats, a dog, and who knows what else to care for. My brother Greg often stayed with us until he got into high school, and he began calling our place "Old McDonald's Farm."

17

Wagon-Wheel Miracle

AFTER BEING ON the farm for one and a half years, we went to visit Bill Barb again. I had another blond-haired, blue-eyed boy, born on October 31, 1973. We named him Edward and called him Eddie. We talked about naming him Paul, after Johnny's brother Paul, who was two years older than Johnny. But Michael insisted we had to name him Eddie. Eddie was Michael's best cousin and twin, the son of Johnny's sister Fannie. So Eddie it was. We were blessed with another contented baby who was well accepted by his brothers and sisters.

From the time she was little, Malinda loved to hold the babies, rocking them and singing to them. I thanked the Lord for her gift with babies, because she was my top baby-sitter. While I was busy with my household and outside chores, Malinda and Susan often babysat the younger children for me. This included not only their younger siblings, but also some other children I babysat while their English mother worked at a job. Elizabeth, however, preferred other tasks to babysitting. If I asked Elizabeth to babysit, she somehow figured out a deal with Malinda to get her to do it.

One day when Malinda was about four, she wanted to hold baby Stephen, so she sneaked into our bedroom where he was lying in his bassinet. The basket part of this bassinet was separate from the legs, and when she was trying to get him out, she ended up dumping him on the floor, with the basket on top of him. I was in the kitchen when I heard Stephen raise a huge racket, crying and wailing, and I came running. I reached under the basket, picked up Stephen, and began soothing him. The noise and the mayhem scared Malinda, and the look on her face let me know that she had finally gotten it through her head that she had to ask before she picked him up to rock him.

***

An even more traumatic accident happened when Malinda was about five and a half years old and our family was out in the field husking corn. Malinda and some other little children I had brought along were in a box underneath the grain wagon. The wagon was slanted so there was enough room for this wooden box where the little ones could crawl in and sit while we were out working in the fields.

"Malinda, go watch the cows in the field so they don't get out in the road," Johnny said. The cows were in a hayfield with no fence, where he had put them out to graze. He didn't want to string up a fence for the week or two they would be there, so they needed to be watched closely. Both Johnny and I thought she had gone to perform her duty, but neither one of us checked to see that she had actually gone.

We were in a high field, had husked all the way back to the back field, and were coming forward toward the barn. It was getting toward noon, and I was thinking it was about time to get some food ready for our dinner. Then, as we were coming down the hill with a full load of corn in the wagon, the horses got a little behind us.

"Giddyup," Johnny said to move the horses beside us, where they needed to be for us to throw the corn into the wagon.

At that same moment, we heard a scream. Startled, we jumped, looked back, and saw little Malinda lying on the ground with the wagon wheel halfway over her stomach.

I screamed just as Johnny said "Giddyup" again.

When Malinda heard her daddy say "Giddyup" the second time, I saw her take a deep breath as if to brace herself. Then the horses pulled the wagon wheel over and off her.

Johnny ran to pick her up, and she was stiff as a board. "I'm taking her to the neighbors," Johnny yelled back to me, running across the field with Malinda in his arms. An English neighbor who had a phone and transportation lived nearby. I just stood there praying and trying not to think of anything else. As Johnny came to a woven wire fence, he started crawling over. He got one leg across, began hefting Malinda over, and suddenly yelled back to me, "She's breathing!" She hadn't been breathing all that time.

"I'm going to bring her back, put her in the box, and take her home." He came back and laid her in the box next to the other children, who had remained in there, frozen with terror. I ran along behind, touching Malinda and talking to her, trying to calm her. We pulled the horses up to the top part of the barn where Johnny tied them, not taking time to unhitch them.

Johnny picked up Malinda, carried her into the house, and laid her on the couch. He ran back outside, jumped bareback onto our riding horse, and rode to our former house, a mile away. That quarter horse went like a flash. As he went flying up the neighbor's driveway, Johnny screamed, "We need help! Malinda is hurt bad."

Our neighbors, Gary and Rose Blythe, were home, and they tore into action. Rose said she had never seen her husband put on his pants so fast in her life. He jumped into their vehicle and raced to our place, but Johnny was back home, off the horse, and in the house before Gary got there. I was shocked he was back so quickly.

While Johnny had gone for help I kneeled beside Malinda as she lay on the couch, gently touching her. Over and over she said in German, "Pretty soon, I cannot breathe anymore." She repeated this probably twenty or thirty times before Johnny got back.

I was full of dread. *We're going to lose her,* I kept thinking. *She is going to die. She's going to die right here.* But soothing words continued to flow out of me, "You're going to be all right. Dad went to get someone." And in my mind, I turned her over to God. I had to let his will be done. Almost immediately Johnny was back, and Gary came to take him and Malinda to the emergency room. I stayed at home with the other children.

They kept Malinda in the hospital for observation until eight o'clock that night. Four to six doctors checked out her stomach, but they could see only one little mark right across her stomach. The wheel had not been high enough on her chest to crush her ribs or low enough to crush her pelvis.

"The ground must have been muddy or very soft," the doctor said, amazed at the apparent lack of damage.

Johnny said, "No, the ground was just normal for October, not muddy or soft."

Malinda and Johnny got home around eight o'clock in the evening, and we laid her on the couch. I got up in the night to check on her, to make sure she was breathing. The next three or four days, I took Malinda to the doctor every day. He checked her stomach each time. Initially it was very hard and bloated, but then it started going down, so he felt we were over the hump. After the third day it was softer, and before long Malinda was up and running around, back to her normal self. Johnny and I were thankful once more for God's blessings and protection. We have seen the hand of the Lord upon each of our children throughout their lives.

Right before Eddie was born, we tore down an old lean-to off the back of our house, which had once been used as a chicken house. It was really dilapidated and dangerous, with the roof caving in and the cement floor pushed up several inches in places from the frost. We knew some snakes were in there, and we wanted to get rid of them, too. Our collie, Rusty, always let us know where the snakes were. He'd bark and bark until we came to look. He often barked around that lean-to until we tore it down.

The next year we added a porch, a basement with a place for butchering, a chimney, and a coal cellar. Before this our coal storage was fairly close to the washing machine, and I didn't like that because of the coal. If a piece of laundry fell on the floor, it got coal dust on it. Then I had to take it to another wash stand to wash it out.

Things went fairly smoothly after Eddie's birth. I'd get up at five o'clock, fix lunches for our three children who were in school, and then go on with my day. I still had lots of diapers to wash, baking, cooking, cleaning, choring, canning, and helping in the fields in summer. When the children were older we planted two thousand strawberry plants. I canned and froze hundreds of quarts of those strawberries. We also sold a lot of them for fifty cents a quart, and we sold sweet corn for fifty cents a dozen. The girls took them to Pep Wayne's on State Route 62, and they sold like hotcakes. The girls made a sign from cardboard, stood right in the yard, and sold our produce to people driving by.

<hr />

I was in a family way again in 1975, and I asked Wayne and Lizzie if I could come to their place to have the baby. Bill Barb's was wonderful, but it was so far to Fredericksburg where they were. I thought it would be easier for Johnny to visit having me closer to home. When I had a baby at Bill Barb's, by the time he got the chores done and got there to visit, it was almost time for him to turn around and go home again. Of course, anybody who knows Lizzie knows she is always willing to help, so she readily agreed.

This time she set up the bed in her upstairs kitchen, because she lived in her basement kitchen in the summer, same as we did. Having no air conditioning, many Amish use basement kitchens during the summer. It's cooler for eating and sleeping, and especially helpful when a person has a lot of canning to do.

On May 4, 1975, we were blessed with a blond-haired, hazel-eyed girl we named Esther. She was named after the daughter of Johnny's brother-in-law Harry and sister Fannie. Harry's Esther was a twin to Eddie. We had chosen the name Esther as a name for a girl when I was expecting Eddie. Michael was really happy with the name. He kept saying, "We have twins like Harry's

Eddie and Esther." My other girls were happy with the name because they liked their cousin Esther. She had a terrific sense of humor, always laughing and telling jokes.

When Esther was two months old and we were still living in our basement kitchen, Mark plopped down on the couch, right on top of where I had laid Esther wrapped in her blanket. Before I could get his attention to tell him to stop, he got up and plopped down again. Esther was lying there sleeping, and he thought she was a pillow. It's a wonder he didn't hurt her. Amazingly, she never even woke up. The youngest babies in our family surely got used to a lot of noise and activity compared to the first ones. Gone were the days when we had to take Michael for a ride before he would go to sleep!

Esther was very contented because she sucked her index finger almost immediately after she was born. She never took a pacifier like most of the rest. Malinda sucked her thumb and was contented, but about the time she was starting to walk, the toy box lid fell on her hand and her thumb got caught in the hinge, cutting a big gash in it. Because I had to bandage it every day for at least a week, she weaned herself from sucking her thumb. But she wouldn't take a pacifier—no way!

In the fall, when Esther was four months old, we had five children going to East Valley School, which was located on Johnny's home farm. Fall was a busy time, with canning, sewing school clothes for the children, cleaning the school, last-minute picnics, silo filling, and corn husking in October. The first year we were on the farm, with Andy's death and getting ready for church at our new home, Johnny never got the corn husked by hand until the day before Christmas. Since it was very late in the year, sometimes it was snowing so hard that I couldn't see the horses and wagon when I looked out the window. I really felt sorry for Johnny, out there by himself all day long for weeks, trying to get it done.

What a worker I had for a husband! He surely loved farming, and he was still able to be at home full time. Only the Lord knew how long that would last. Sometimes it's a blessing not to see into the future.

18

Feeding a Family of Twelve

I WAS EXPECTING another baby in August of 1976, but in March of that year my hernia was very, very bad. To make the burning pain go away, I often had to stop and pull my knee up to my stomach, or else I had to sit down. Dr. Eberly said this had to be my last pregnancy or my health would suffer even more. Johnny and I talked it over, weighing seriously what the doctor had said, our love for children, and our faith. We sadly decided this had to be our last baby, and that I would have a tubal ligation soon after this baby was born. It was a hard decision because I really loved babies, but with the shape I was in, we felt this was what we had to do.

I asked the doctor if I could go to Lizzie's again for this birth because of the convenience for Johnny, the tender care from Lizzie, and to save expenses. Dr. Eberly agreed, but said, "If I am at Bill Barb's for a delivery when your time comes, you will be left with only Johnny and Lizzie to deliver the baby." Johnny was not very happy about that possibility, but we talked it over and agreed to take our chances and go forward with the delivery at Lizzie's.

On August 12, 1976, we were blessed with our sixth son. Thankfully, Dr. Eberly was there to deliver him since no one was ready to deliver at Barb's. This baby was born on my cousin Davy's birthday. By this time, Davy had become a cowboy out west.

Johnny and I had been thinking about Paul as a name again, but we hadn't really decided on anything by the time of birth. The night our baby was born, Johnny's brother Pep Wayne had a dream in which we named our little son Matthew. In the morning Pep Wayne asked me, "Did you and Johnny decide on a name?"

"No," I said. "He'll be back tonight and we'll probably decide then."

"Well, I had a dream last night that you named this little son Matthew," Wayne said.

Matthew? We had not even considered that name.

When Johnny came to visit later that night, I said, "Well, did we decide on a name? Is it going to be Paul?"

What Johnny said next was very surprising to me. "I was in the field today, and it was like I heard a voice from God say, 'Name him Matthew,'" Johnny said. Even though we had never discussed the name Matthew at all, now it seemed to us that God was talking and we were listening.

Johnny and I decided that, with the two confirmations we had, our new little son must be named Matthew. Right from the beginning we told Matthew, "God has a plan for you." And we have told him that throughout his life.

The boys at home were glad this baby was a boy, but the girls had wanted another girl to even up our family.

One woman in our church even told me, "I think Eddie was supposed to be a girl."

"Why do you think that?" I asked.

She answered, "Because every other child was a different sex up until Eddie."

So after I had Matthew, I would tell people I have ten children. And then I would rattle them off—boy, girl, boy, girl, boy, girl, boy, boy, girl, boy. Some people thought it was funny that I could rattle them off so fast. Sometimes I still do it today.

My mom was very happy to know that this was our last baby. She and Dad offered to take care of him at their place when I went to the hospital for my tubal. When I went into the hospital to have my operation, the doctor said, "It's a good idea to have your appendix removed during the operation."

"No thanks," I answered, perplexed. I was coming in for a tubal and wondered why he was talking about removing my appendix.

He said, "Well, I hope I don't see you in another couple of weeks or so. Almost every time I do a tubal, the woman comes back a few weeks later to have her appendix out." So I agreed to have my appendix out during my tubal operation. Things seemed to go fine, and after a few days I was back home with my recovery coming along.

One week after the operation I was sewing clothes for our school children for their Christmas program. I liked to make sure my children had new clothes to wear when they stood up front for the Christmas program. After sitting at the treadle sewing machine for hours and hours for days on end, I got a terrible bladder infection that lasted for months. Each time, I went to the doctor and got an antibiotic, but as soon as that round was finished, back it came again.

One day an Amish woman near Fredericksburg looked into my eyes and said, "Oh! Your colon is all impacted. You've got to get that colon cleansed and then your infection will clear up." She gave me something like clay in a bag, red beet juice, and some aloe vera. "Take these several times a day and fast for the next ten days, drinking only red beet juice."

I was desperate to get some relief, so I followed her orders, and amazingly my bladder infection went away. Not only did it go away, but I didn't have any more bladder infections for years. I knew I was on to something; I was beginning to learn about natural ways to heal my body.

Mom told me Dad had a wonderful time with Matthew while I was in the hospital. I cannot remember Dad having a wonderful time with any of us children or any of my other children. Mom said, "Your dad played with Matthew. He would hold Matthew up and rub their foreheads together."

Marlene's mother, Margaret, at age seventy-five, at Marlene's home. Photograph taken Christmas 1993.

"Really!" I said. "I can't believe it." It was hard for me to believe that he enjoyed one of the children. There was no end to my surprise when she said she enjoyed watching Mark, too, when she took care of him while I had Malinda. Mark took his first steps during that week, and I was so sorry I missed it. I wanted to see all my children's first steps and enjoy every new phase of their lives.

Matthew, Esther, and Eddie never got to really know my father, because he lost a courageous battle with cancer one year later in August 1977. He was only sixty-one. When I last visited him in the hospital, tears rolled down his cheeks as I told him about how happy I was being married to Johnny and being Amish. "You can count yourself proud that I married an Amish man," I told my father on that last visit. "I am so glad that I accepted Jesus Christ when I was young. I have peace and joy."

Mom was left a widow at age fifty-eight. When I think of Dad's death, I think of 1 Corinthians 15:55-57: "O death, where is thy sting? O grave, where is thy victory? The sting of death is sin; and the strength of sin is the law. But thanks be to God, which giveth us the victory through our Lord Jesus Christ."

⊷━━━━━━━⊶

I had a Swartzentruber Amish girl, Saloma Byler, for my hired girl that summer. She came in June and lived with us all summer. Stephen, in his cute little baby talk, called her "Lonesome Me." She only went home on weekends, even though she lived just a mile and a half away. Michael was old enough, and now skilled enough with the horse and buggy, that he could go get her after her weekends at home. Sometimes if Saloma couldn't come, one of her sisters came instead. Saloma worked very hard that summer. Besides working in the garden and house, she milked and worked in the fields. The children really loved her, and I was grateful for her help.

That year I kept track of what I put up into jars with Saloma's help. With the meat I canned in the winter and the produce we canned that summer and fall, I had over two thousand quarts of canned goods. The shelves in our basement storage room couldn't hold them all! I had to put many jars on the floor. I did four hundred quarts of applesauce, and all of my canned fruit had sugar in it. I have never canned that much again. Often I made notes of my cooking and canning in my cookbook. Here are some excerpts I recently came across:

> **Nov. 12, 1979**—Lizzie and Lizzie Raber, her neighbor, came to help butcher 20 roosters and 25 old hens. Canned 24 quarts crumb meat and 16 2-quart jars of whole pieces from the roosters, used for frying or roasting.

> **Dec. 15, 1979**—butchered 4 big hogs, took pork chops from 2 hogs, 40 lbs sausage, 3 big cake pans of *Ponhaus* [scrapple—see recipes at end of book] to our locker in the Kidron Store. I canned 25 qt. of sausage, 15 qt. of chunk meat from the shoulders, 6 qt. pork chops, the hams and bacons were immersed in a salt brine, bacon a week or so, hams 6 weeks, then smoked in our smokehouse.

> **Dec. 28, 1979**—Bro. Paul came to help J shoot and skin a young beef for us. After letting it hang for 3 days in the upper part of the cold barn, J & I cut up the beef. The next day I canned 100 qt. of hamburger, 32 qt. of beef chunks, 11 qt. of steaks, and 18 pts. of steaks that were fried in oil, gave 12 lbs to friends, and kept 12 lbs of hamburger for us.

What I canned in 1981. 150 qt. Strawberries, 266 qt. of applesauce, 60 qt. sweet corn, 44 qt. of big black cherries, 15 qt. of green beans, 166 qt. of peaches, 15 qt. of bread-and-butter pickles, 84 qt. of tomato juice, 18 qt. of pizza sauce, 30 qt. of veg. soup (about couldn't get the children to eat that either), 14 qt. of pears, 7 pt. of ketchup, 5 batches of strawberry jam ["not enough," I wrote beside this entry], 8 batches of elderberry jam, 10 batches of blackberry jam.

During canning, when I needed more sugar, the kids and I sold corn or fruit. Around our place we picked raspberries, cherries, and elderberries. When the children turned a couple of years older, they helped pick blackberries at the Buckeye Beagle Club where my dad used to run his beagles. A lot of elderberries still grew on our farm, left from the previous owner, and we picked and sold them to a restaurant in a nearby town for pies. They paid us when we delivered the fruit. Then we went straight to the store to buy more sugar in big twenty-five-pound sacks so the canning could go on.

Sugar, sugar, sugar—I used a lot of sugar when I canned fruit. Sugar is cheap and it surely cheapens the body, but I didn't know it at the time. Now that I know more about what sugar does to the body and to the immune system, I think it's no wonder I was always tired with all the sugar we ate—not only in our canned foods, but also in our pies, cakes, and cookies, too.

It took a lot of food each day to keep our big family fed. Often for dinner I used eight pounds of potatoes, peeled, cooked, and mashed, or ten pounds for French fries; two or three quarts of meat; one quart of vegetables; and two or three quarts of apple-sauce or rhubarb sauce. We topped that off with a gallon or two of milk, so it was fortunate we had cows. In the summer we used even more milk, averaging about three gallons a day, because we ate a lot of cold milk soup. An Amish staple, cold milk soup has bread in the bottom of a bowl covered with whatever fruit is in season or handy, like bananas or berries, sprinkled with sugar, and milk poured over it all. This was an easy and refreshing meal that often came in handy when we were busy canning or in the fields for long hours. I didn't care for cold milk soup and neither did Susan, so I made us sandwiches.

I never could make nice, soft bread, so we bought most of it. Each week we used, on average, eighteen loaves of bread and two to three pounds of butter. In the winter I made bacon and eggs for breakfast, but in the summer we ate more milk and cereal, which came to about eight boxes of cereal a week.

In the winter my favorite pastime was reading. I read the Bible, non-fiction books, and novels. Johnny's favorites were the Bible and Zane Gray and Louis L'Amour westerns. I think he read almost every book Zane Gray and Louis L'Amour wrote.

The winter of 1977 was a record year for bad weather. I wrote:

Sunday, January 17, 1977—We're having a terrible blizzard. Went to John Levi's for church. 23° below 0. That's a record around here! The drinking cups for the cows were frozen this morn. Children stayed home from school. Window on back porch busted out from wind.

Friday, January 28, 1977—No school yesterday or today, because of another blizzard. Drifted shut a little down the road, and also drifted shut at the crossroad Wed. night. Couldn't go today to the Dr. with Matthew and Esther.

Thursday, January 26, 1978—below 0 blizzard, so Johnny came home at noon. He had to walk from blacktop. Children will sleep down tonight. I'm having puffballs or farmer's buttons, as some Amish call them, tonight for supper.

Farmer's buttons are much like homemade donuts, but are made with flour, sugar, eggs, milk, and leavening (baking powder) instead of yeast. Hot chocolate and a bunch of these make a nice supper meal on a cold winter night.

These buttons make me think of another favorite meal, which I would make once or twice in the summer when making and canning my fresh applesauce. *Dampf Knepp* (buttons, or caramel dumplings) are delicious. They are made with yeast, very similar to bread dough. With trail-style bologna and Swiss cheese held in the other hand, a person had a meal fit for a queen.

Both of these recipes (see pages 247–51) came from my *Mennonite Community Cookbook*, which Lizzie bought for me early on in my marriage. Now the pages are spattered and worn, because I used that book very much all through raising my family. It was a wonderful, old-fashioned book. Each chapter showed some aspect of Mennonite life, including stories about butchering day, and doing the chickens, and baking at Christmas. Many nights I sat and read the stories, again and again, and looked at all the interesting pictures. I passed many enjoyable evenings with this well-used friend.

19

An Amish Wedding

AFTER FIVE YEARS of farming our hundred acres and staying at home, Johnny had to start working the day shift at L-P again. We needed more income. We all felt terrible about it, but many times in life a person has to do things he doesn't want to. Even though Johnny was away working, and the children and I missed him so much, I consoled myself that at least he was away working to make a better life for us. He wasn't out doing wicked stuff.

Johnny cleaned the cow stables every day, but with his job it was difficult for him to do everything he was used to doing on the farm. To save him time, I sometimes hauled the manure out on a wheelbarrow and piled it where he could remove it later. Many times Michael and Mark harnessed the horses after they came home from school, and then Johnny used the manure spreader, digging into that pile and spreading it out in the fields. In the winter we never ate supper until after chores, anywhere from seven to nine o'clock in the evening.

Every morning before going to work at L-P, Johnny would say, "I wish it was my last day to work there." But that didn't happen for twenty-seven years. He worked there thirty-two years altogether, including the five years he worked there before farming full time. When he retired from L-P, we teased him that he'd finally got a real job, because then he started working as a skidder operator in the woods.

In the winter months the children played Ping-Pong, checkers, cards, and other games. In the summer they played softball, volleyball, and badminton, and rode horses a lot. All our children learned to swim and ride horses.

Michael, Mark, and Elizabeth rode an old white horse called Penny to school, all three riding her together. She had a knee with very bad arthritis, and she limped with every step she took, which made her very slow. But the children didn't care as long as they didn't have to walk. My dad gave Penny to them because he felt sorry that they had such a long walk to school. I thought it was very nice of him to have pity on them and to do something so nice.

Michael, Mark, and Elizabeth in 1973, riding their horse, Penny, to East Valley School.

We'll retrace our steps back again to the January 26, 1978, blizzard, when I begged Johnny not to go to work in the morning. Being the responsible man he was, he said, "If the driver shows up, I'm going." The driver came, and off he went. Some hours later he reappeared in the kitchen, and we didn't recognize him. His face looked like a red, dried-up apple. His stocking cap and denim pants were almost frozen onto him. The girls helped him out of them, but his cap and pants were so icy they stood on the floor by themselves. Seeing him, we had to laugh, but when he told us what had happened we found out it was really no laughing matter.

He and the other men in his vehicle had to dig the driver's truck and some other cars out of huge snowdrifts, and then Johnny ended up walking a mile in that storm to get home. He said, "I couldn't see my hand in front of my face, it was snowing so hard." The temperature was still below zero. He spent a lot of time in the barn that evening, stuffing bags and straw into every crack and cranny to keep out the snow and cold. We later heard from some of our English neighbors that the wind chill was one hundred degrees below zero.

That winter another incident happened: our buggy tipped over on its side. The snow was so exceptional, with such big drifts, that our children took the buggy to school. On the way, the buggy tipped over. The horse patiently stood there while the kids opened the storm front and piled out into the snow. Then they righted the buggy and went on to school.

There are so many incidents and accidents that happened to our children going to or from school that I can't recount them all here.

Our children have many happy memories of East Valley School, but I'm sorry to say they also have some sad ones. I have already related Michael's problem with being teased. Another time, our son Mark was pulled out of his seat by his ear by the teacher, which was upsetting to me. He got such an ear infection that he couldn't go to school for a week. My children weren't perfect—I, their mother, certainly knew that. But to pull a boy's ear to get his whole body off the seat is uncalled for, in my opinion.

Our children were teased a lot at school by the other children. We couldn't buy our children more than one set of boots, one pair of church shoes, and their school shoes. Sometimes they didn't get their pair of school shoes at the beginning of the school year until it got cool. One of our children even had duct tape on his shoes to hold the sole on the front so it didn't flop. Many times when they got new shoes, the other children at school tramped on them and then acted as though they hadn't seen their feet.

We couldn't afford new bicycles, so we bought used bikes for our children one year. But the very first day they had them, as our children were getting ready to come home, a boy took a baseball bat and destroyed the seat on one of them.

Once I made Valentine cookies for the whole school. Later, my girls came home crying and said, "You know what some girls did? They took their cookies and just crumbled them up in front of us and threw them away." Some of the older girls had waited until my girls were leaving to go home. Then they showed my girls that they hadn't eaten their cookies because they didn't like them. They threw the cookies away right in front of them and laughed. If any of my girls happened to have a rip in their dress, the other children made fun of them. It was very hard for me when my children came home and told me about these problems.

Some children could be so mean and cruel, while others were so very nice. There were other incidents when our youngest children went to school, but I will say that these children are now grown and some of them have apologized and asked for forgiveness for their bad behavior, which was freely given. If we could only forgive and forget like our Lord does, our lives would be much easier and more blessed. But we are human and often it takes time for us to work through learning these lessons.

When I was young, I felt sorry for the children in my grade school who were very poor. Some of them didn't have socks or warm coats to wear in the winter. I had compassion for them, just as I had for some of the children in my neighborhood, and I tried to instill that same compassion into my children.

Of all my children, Stephen had the hardest time in school. It seemed he was always thinking of something stupid to do. I really think he did many of these naughty things because he wanted attention. He would even smile while he did something wrong. The thing that usually got him into trouble was the fact that he couldn't say no. At home he would be the first to jump if I asked him to do something for me, but he was also the first to do dumb stunts at school.

───────

Our family took what opportunities we could for fun and recreation together. The children enjoyed the hot-dog roasts we had every Sunday evening during the summer. With Johnny working away from home five days a week, and with a big family, we didn't go away much. Johnny also wanted to be at church on Sunday or stay at home on our off Sundays. He hardly ever missed church services. It was and still is very important to him.

Sometimes we took our old hack and horse and went up to the woods to have a picnic and swing on grapevines. I even did it! It was fun. Often on Sunday evenings we played volleyball, because we had enough people in our family to do it. There are some advantages to having a large family!

On the Fourth of July we loved to take the children to Mount Eaton to watch the fireworks. We tried to get a driver with a pickup for this outing so that the children could sit on bales of straw in the back to watch the show. Many times we promised them this treat if they got finished shocking the wheat, so they worked extra hard and fast. This was one of the highlights of the summer for them.

Another summer we promised them a big trampoline if they did the shocking well. Johnny and I said to them, "If you do your work well, do what you're supposed to do at the time you're supposed to do it, and don't complain, we will get you a trampoline. Wouldn't that be a good incentive for you to work this year?" The kids had been waiting to get a trampoline; they had asked for one for a couple of years. They had jumped on one several times at someone else's house, and they really wanted one.

That summer and fall they all worked very hard, and we stuck to our promise. They were so excited when we brought their trampoline home that we could barely get the thing put together before they were all on it. Eddie had already learned to do flips. He was our best trampoliner, but they all loved it. This was a very good investment for us, as the children used it for years. It got so much use that occasionally we had to buy more springs or put on a new pad.

Our children worked hard, but they also played hard. They loved to swing on big hay ropes from trees on the lawn. Esther had begged Johnny for a couple of years to put a swing out on the lawn. She finally said, "I'm almost going to be too big before I get a swing." There was an old electric pole left from when the former English owners had installed electricity in the house. So Johnny put up another pole and crosspiece, and attached a big swing for her to swing right on our lawn.

In the summer of 1977, I decided to try riding a horse again because I wasn't pregnant and wouldn't be having any more children. Since I used to ride my cousin's horse when I lived in Beach City, I thought, *I know how to do this. It will be no problem.*

Well, there was a problem: I was a whole lot heavier than I was as a young girl. The riding went fine, but when I went to get off, the cinch was too loose, the saddle went sideways, and I fell with my left leg under me. I tore the ligament and tendon in my ankle, and was laid up for a long time. It's been over thirty years since that accident, but I still have problems in my left leg. That was the end of my horse-riding days. I drove the horse and buggy to the store in Wilmot, and to the neighbors when I needed to help them get ready for church. But as soon as my girls could take me, I quit driving.

Some things I never could do. I didn't trust myself—and Johnny didn't either—to mow hay with the mower or to use a grain binder. I couldn't back the horses and wagon. I couldn't put the forks into loose hay to put in the hay mow. I couldn't spread the hay out in the mow. Being raised English, I didn't have the knowledge and skills to do many of these tasks. But each one of our children could do all of these necessary things for running a farm. When our English neighbors gave us their pony and cart, Wayne was the one to drive it. Wayne thought he was the pro and wouldn't let Mark drive. Wayne still likes to drive horses.

When Michael was sixteen he wanted to work away from home, but we told him he had to wait until he was seventeen. Then he got a job with Jonas (nicknamed "Giggles") Yoder, who worked in construction. Michael gave us almost all his money from that job until he was eighteen. That money paid for a buggy shop with a basement, which we badly needed. We really thanked the Lord for this, and Michael felt good knowing he paid for the shop.

When he was seventeen, Michael started dating. After some heartbreaks with an Amish girl, he decided to date our neighbor girl Martha, who was Mennonite. We did not approve of him dating a girl outside our faith, and I'm sure her parents didn't approve either. When Elizabeth was dating age, Michael said she could only date boys he approved. He didn't listen to *us* about our choices in dating, but Elizabeth was supposed to listen to *him*!

In her later teen years, Elizabeth cleaned houses and caught chickens at night for chicken growers in our neighborhood. She got to keep all the money from these jobs. Catching chickens was a very physical job. She caught the chickens by the legs, and put four in her left hand and another three in her right. Then she went to the truck, lifted her armfuls of squawking, flapping chickens high above her head, handed them to the person with the truck, and he put them in cages. It was exhausting physical labor. Sometimes Elizabeth and some of our other children went in the evening, after all the day's work and the evening chores and supper were over, and worked catching chickens until midnight. Even though it was hard work they did it willingly, because this was a way they could make some money.

Their arms would get very tired after catching hundreds of chickens and putting them into cages on big semis. One day Elizabeth said, "Nick Orrie's Danny really helped me last night. He took my chickens from me and handed them up to the guy to put in the cages."

"Yeah, Nick Orrie's Danny was helping Elizabeth," Malinda chimed in. "What do you think of that?"

Well, I knew what I thought of that, and later I said to Johnny, "You know what? I bet you that Danny will be here soon to have a date with Elizabeth."

I had a gut feeling about why he was helping her, and it turned out I was right. Not too many months later, Elizabeth and Danny were steadies. Michael approved of Danny, so I figured it was all right. Michael knew Danny well because they had worked together catching chickens, and he could see that Danny was a real worker.

When she was seventeen, Elizabeth got a job at L-P where Johnny worked, so she was able to ride to work with her dad. She grew up more after that, because she worked with older English women who didn't take great care of what came out of their mouths. But she knew right from wrong, and she told me, "Boy, those women shouldn't be talking the way they do."

In the fall of 1983, Elizabeth said she and Danny wanted to get married the next year. To get ready for our first Amish wedding meant a lot of changes had to be made. We had talked for a couple of years about remodeling the house, because our family was growing and our house didn't have enough room for us all. When all twelve of us were in our living room at one time, it was crowded. It took a large space for all of us.

In the fall and winter of 1983–84 we had Jonas Miller, a carpenter, remodel our house for the second time. We wanted a larger living room and a larger kitchen. We took out the old bathroom and made a much larger and nicer one by combining a hallway and the small bedroom—not much bigger than a closet—that Johnny and I had made do with all these years. We added a larger bedroom with more windows for us. I loved windows for their light and view, and since the new bedroom faced north, we felt it would be okay to put windows in there since we hardly ever got wind from that direction. We also planned to put a patio out back because we had patio doors off the living room.

But during the summer we decided that instead of adding a patio we would just add another room off the back for sewing and activities. As we talked about changing the plans from a patio to a room, Johnny mentioned, "If anything ever happened to one of us, that's where the viewing could be." We never thought anything like that would happen so soon.

Last of all, after eleven years I got a nice, big front porch. Finally I had a place to put our swing—the same swing we had over at our mini-farm. It was the same swing on which the children and I sang and cried because I missed my husband and they missed their father.

Sitting in the swing brought back many memories. Reflecting back on those days—days that seemed so long and hard at times, with their loneliness and hard-learned lessons of a new life—I thought about how the years had sped by. Life is such a vapor, and it is such a short time that we tarry here on earth.

Along with the remodeling we started planning for a fall wedding. We had so many questions, so many details to attend to. Who would be the couple's witnesses? Who and how many cooks and table waiters? At an Amish wedding, the bride's church is automatically invited, but how many other guests to invite? Where would the wedding church be? Would there be enough room? Today there are kitchens on wheels, which many Amish people rent for these occasions, but back then there was no such thing. Whatever was needed in the kitchen was borrowed from neighbors and relatives. I had not had a nice wedding, so I was glad to make the best weddings I could for my daughters. But during all the planning and preparations, an occasional doubt would creep in: *Oh, can I do this?* I marvel to think I went from being a small-town girl, cooking for five or six, to cooking for hundreds in one day. Of course, I had lots of help, too.

Elizabeth decided to have her brother Mark as a witness. Michael didn't want to be a witness, probably because he was going steady with Martha, who was Mennonite. Danny had one of his cousins, Paul Yoder, as his witness, because he was the only boy and the baby in the family. His six sisters were all married.

The biggest expenses for an Amish wedding are the food, gifts for the cooks and table waiters, and fabric to make clothes for the family: dresses, pants, shirts, and aprons. We prepared food on Saturday, Monday, Tuesday, and Wednesday before the wedding, which was on Thursday, October 4, 1984. We kept the food cold in two big containers filled with three to four hundred pounds of ice borrowed from the Pep Waynes. We also used my icebox (I think that's the year I first got an icebox) and our spring water. About 300 to 350 people came to the wedding, and we fed them twice. Some of the older people weren't invited to supper, which we called the young people's dinner.

We set up lots and lots of tables for the dinner. There were tables in the kitchen, the living room, on our enclosed patio, and in the basement. The wedding church was in the top portion of our shop. Besides the many church people, my relatives and friends were also invited. When the day finally came, all went well. It was a beautiful fall day and everyone was happy, especially Elizabeth and Danny. Of course, Johnny and I had some times of reflection and sadness, thinking back to when Elizabeth was little, nevermore to be our little girl whom we had loved, raised, and protected for nineteen years.

Michael ended up having a part in the wedding after all. He was called a *Hostler*, which means a helper to hitch and unhitch the people's horses and do other odd jobs that needed to be done, like carrying buckets of water and milk. Martha was one of three table waiters at the corner table, which was the bridal table at which the married couple and their witnesses sat.

The night after the wedding, I woke up with a terrible migraine, probably from nerves and overeating. This happened after all my girls' weddings. Our new son-in-law Danny said he thought he'd had headaches until he heard me that night, moaning and groaning until I finally threw up. He used to have migraines, but when he heard what I went through, he decided there are people who had worse headaches than he did. Danny heard me in the night because the married couple often spends the wedding night in the bride's home. Elizabeth, being the oldest girl, had her own bedroom. The couple is needed to help with the work of cleaning up, tearing down, and returning borrowed things the next day. There are many board tables to tear down and lots of roaster pans, serving bowls, and dishes to return to friends and relatives. Once everything is back in place after the wedding, if there is time to move the newly married couple's furniture into their new place, well and good. Some young people stay at the parents' home a week or two longer, if they have to wait for the person or family to move out of the place where they will be living.

Having our first Amish wedding was a lot of work, but we had much help, and these types of events keep our community closely knit. When it came time for my girls' weddings, we did it all with the help of our family and friends. I didn't have anything catered. Some people came at four or five in the morning to begin frying the chicken. Then we all worked together, cooking, baking, and preparing the place. That's what we spend money for: eats for the Amish wedding!

Some of the men told me they loved coming to our home for my girls' weddings. They said they enjoyed it more than any wedding they ever went to. It couldn't have been that they enjoyed talking with me, because I was a nervous wreck from all the cooking, planning, and just plain hard work over several days. But they loved our place, loved the location, the hospitality, and good food.

Nowadays they don't do Amish wedding dinners like they used to, with everything home cooked. It seems people get all stressed out, and they have much of the food catered. They even get all the cakes catered, and, as I mentioned, now you can rent a kitchen. Some single girls bought into a business that provides a kitchen on wheels for rent, which comes equipped with extra dishes, a couple of stoves, some sinks to which you can hook up a hose, and special chicken fryers. This shows the ingenuity of the Amish and makes things much easier on the bridal family.

After the wedding Danny and Elizabeth moved to the Nick Orrie farm, Danny's home place, and farmed for about one year. Because the farm was too big for just the two of them to farm with horses, they hired our son Wayne as a helper.

Michael liked to visit Danny and Elizabeth. The last time she rode with and talked to him was the first week in November, when they both voted for the first time. By the next week, he was fighting to stay alive in Mercy Hospital.

20

A Tragic Accident

IF ONLY WE could keep our children sheltered and out of harm's way. Ever since our oldest son, Michael, had started driving a vehicle, I feared a knock on the door in the middle of the night telling us something tragic had happened. That fear became a reality on November 12, 1984, at one in the morning. An hour earlier there had been an accident.

That evening, a nineteen-year-old boy took our son to a bar for a pool tournament. Michael had met this young man at the truck cap manufacturing plant, where they worked together for a couple of months. We had never met this boy, but his dad had gone to the same Amish church as Johnny when they were boys. His mother was English and had been in my grade in school, but we were not close acquaintances. So it was very shocking when this woman came to our door at one in the morning.

"How old is Michael?" she asked me. "There has been a terrible accident near Sugarcreek."

"Twenty-one," I told her, confused by the strange question. "How bad is your son?" I asked, thinking they were together in the car.

She looked embarrassed when she said her son wasn't with Michael. She explained her need for Michael's age: "They can't really do anything with him until they know his age."

Johnny and I said to each other, "Why didn't they find his billfold and get his age from that?" We couldn't really understand what was going on. Michael never left his billfold at home. These and other questions started flooding our minds, and we were kind of dazed. So we asked her to call a driver for us, as the nearest telephone was a half mile away.

With heavy hearts and still in shock, Johnny and I dressed for the trip to the hospital. We sat in tremendous anxiety as we waited for the driver to come, not knowing the condition of our son. We waited and waited and waited, but no vehicle came. I thought we would go crazy. We kept saying over and over, "How could this have happened? *How* could this have happened? If this boy wasn't with him, how could Michael be in an accident?" We were so confused and kept saying things like, "It just doesn't make sense." "He went with this boy, and yet the mother said there's been a terrible accident." "Where was her son? He was the one driving, the one with the car. What could have happened?" "Why didn't she offer to take us to the hospital?"

While we sat there the children came out, awakened by the noise and wondering what had happened. Soon the whole household was in an uproar. All the kids came to the living room, asking questions for which we had very few answers, talking and crying as they heard that Michael had been in an accident. Finally, after waiting several hours, Johnny went to the phone himself to call a driver.

Someone had called the driver, but somehow the driver had understood that he was to go to the hospital, not to our house. When he arrived at the hospital, he asked for John and Marlene Miller, saying, "I'm supposed to take them home. Something about their son being hurt."

"Oh, maybe you can identify this boy," the hospital workers said.

He was flabbergasted. "Me? What do you want me to do?"

"Please come with us. All we know is this boy's name is supposed to be Mike. Will you come and identify him? Since you were hired to pick up Johnny and Marlene Miller, maybe his last name is Miller."

The driver, Ross Artman, went into the room and almost fell over looking at the horrible condition of the person lying there. He said, "I cannot positively tell you if this is Michael Miller because he is so swollen and bruised. Michael is about this age and build, but I just can't identify him." Then, finally, he realized that he needed to come to our house and take us to the hospital.

Because of this and many miscommunications, we didn't get to the hospital until six o'clock in the morning. When we finally arrived, we couldn't recognize our son. He was in a coma, and his head was swollen and bruised. Johnny took his hand and started rubbing it and his arm. "Mom and Dad are here. It's okay. We're right beside you." At that reassuring touch from his father and those tender words, Michael's heart rate came down, so we knew he heard us.

But there was so much brain damage that the neurosurgeon didn't expect him to live through the day. "His heart is beating so fast that it will give out soon at this pace," he said. "Is he a laid-back boy or a fighter?"

We both knew our son very well. "A fighter and very athletic," we replied. "That alone may keep him alive," the doctor said. "If his heart stops or if he needs a breathing machine, do you want us to resuscitate him?"

"Of course," we said. "Yes."

The nurses told us we could have anyone we wanted to visit Michael in ICU, as they were sure the end was near. To their surprise, he lived eight and a half days. More than two hundred people, old and young, came to the ICU to see him during that time. The nurses remarked that he surely must have been well liked.

Michael's first cousin Eddie was there at the hospital every day. From the time he heard about Michael's accident, he came and he never left us. He even slept at the hospital on the floor. About the fourth day in the early afternoon, Eddie said, "I just have to go home to help Dad do the chores." He lived on a farm, and they had lots of cows. He knew others were doing his share of the chores. "When I get my chores done, I'll be back."

"That's okay honey, you go home. We understand," we told him. Even with this terrible tragedy, our own farmwork still had to be done. Later when we were talking with some people, lo and behold, there was Eddie. "Eddie, you didn't go home and chore already and come back? That's not possible. You haven't been gone long enough," Johnny said.

"I can't leave Michael," Eddie answered. "I have to be here." During those eight and a half days, we cannot remember him ever going home. Eddie was Michael's best cousin, his best buddy, and he was there for him. He said, "If I ever get married and have a boy, his name will be Michael." He later did have only one son, and he named him Michael.

Johnny's brother Wayne also came to the hospital every day. He spent hours reading Scripture to Michael and praying over him. In the darkest hours of Michael's fight for his life, his uncle prayed over and over, "Jesus, have mercy on him."

Many, many others were so kind and caring during this difficult and tragic time in our lives. A man from Dover who worked for the gas company gave us a telephone credit card and told us to use it to "call anyone you want, especially anyone you want to have pray for Michael." This was a blessing for us and we used it mostly to call my English relatives and friends, as our Amish friends didn't have telephones. My great-aunt and uncle were there every day, buying meals for Johnny and me to make sure that we kept up our strength. They even offered to pay for Michael's care in Akron or Cleveland if we thought he could get better care there. We can never thank these relatives and friends enough for all their caring and giving during this time.

Bit by bit, the story came to us, and we began to piece together a picture of the night of the accident. It is much more complex and mysterious than I can recount. The young man with Michael didn't want to go home when Michael did, and he let Michael take his car. Soon after Michael left, the young man decided that he did indeed want to go home. So his girlfriend took him. On the way home, they actually ran into this young man's car, which Michael had been driving— but Michael had already apparently had a terrible accident by the time they arrived. The young man and some other people found Michael lying in a ditch not far from the car. Michael was first transported to Union Hospital in Dover, then transferred to Mercy Hospital in Canton. We still didn't know what had caused the accident.

During Michael's second day in the hospital, I went to pray in the chapel just down the hall from his room. I went there that one time only. When I walked in, I saw crucifixes and icons, and I felt such a coldness. I kept thinking, *Pray, Marlene. You came here to pray.* I put my head down and nothing came. I looked up, looked around, and just shivered—so cold and strange it looked and seemed to me. I put my head down again and tried to pray, but nothing came to mind. Finally I knew, *You've got to get out of here. This is not the place.*

Looking back down the hallway, I went into the bathroom, and it came to me: *This is the place. This is the only quiet place in the hospital where I can feel peace and pray.* In the waiting room there were TVs on and people coming in and out. So I went into the bathroom many, many times, and that is where I did my praying. It was a quiet place where I could concentrate and pour my heart out to God.

But those were difficult times of prayer. Oh, how I prayed for God to heal my son, to help my son, to save my son. But how hard it was to say, "Thy will be done." Many times I wrestled with my feelings and with God's will in that bathroom, trying to understand what this terrible trial was all about.

The third day he was in the hospital, still in a coma and unresponsive, we had Michael anointed. The bishop and preachers from our church came and touched his hair with some anointing oil as they prayed. Desperately, I prayed my own prayer. "God, give me a sign that Michael knows he's being anointed, even if I'm the only one to see or hear it." Incredibly, as we watched, Michael turned his head from one side to the other as soon as the oil touched his hair, and then he let out a long sigh. I cried and cried, thankful that God had let me see this confirmation. I felt his sins were forgiven by the Lord at this time, and my heart overflowed with gratitude: "Thank you again, Lord, for the gift of forgiveness and mercy." That precious time was like a little island of calm in the storm that engulfed us day after day.

Those eight long days were a roller-coaster ride for us. One day our hopes were raised that Michael would survive, but the next they were dashed. This time was very hard on our other children, also, as they could not all come to the hospital and be with Michael every day. Some of them only got to come a few times, because we had a dairy farm and the chores had to be done. Our children cried often at school, and the teacher had a difficult time understanding the depth of their grief. Of course she couldn't understand it; she had never experienced anything like what our children were going through.

We hardly slept or ate during those days. We couldn't figure what had caused Michael's accident until the state highway patrol told us he had been drinking alcohol. However, the EMT and others on the squad said, "He threw up something like fries and a cheeseburger, but very little liquid." So we questioned what the patrol had to say about alcohol being the cause. The questions kept piling up as we heard many conflicting reports, but no answers came.

On the seventh day they put Michael on kidney dialysis, trying to work the gas and fluid out of him. They let us look at him before they put him on dialysis. To my mother's heart, the room seemed so cold, and he had nothing but a sheet over his midsection.

This was their last resort, the doctor said. "If this doesn't work, there's nothing more we can do. Let's hope for the best." But the best did not happen. Michael was only on the machine two hours before blood started coming out of his nose, mouth, and ears from the blood thinner they gave him for the dialysis. Who could believe this was happening to our son—our son who had been so fit and healthy?

The neurosurgeon said that even though the MRIs were showing Michael's brain was improving, the experimental drug they had given him for the brain swelling was wreaking havoc on his bowels and kidneys. It turned out it wasn't the brain injury that killed him but uremic poisoning, which turned him a light green color.

When blood started coming out all those different places, the doctor came to the waiting room shaking his head. He said, "We have tried everything and nothing seems to be working. Michael is dying. There's nothing more we can do for him." Oh, the anguish those words brought, a deeper blow than any physical pain could cause.

On that eighth day, I *had* to give up. All those times in the hospital bathroom I had wrestled with God, prayed to him to save my son, and struggled with God's will. But now I knew I had to accept the worst. I had to accept the fact that I was losing my son, but I couldn't accept that this was God's perfect will. Even as I submitted to the inevitable and finally said, "Thy will be done," it would only be much later that I came to understand about God's perfect will and God's permissive will.

On Wednesday evening, at 7:30 p.m., only Michael's girl-friend, Martha, and her mother remained in the room with Johnny and me. All our children and some other visitors had been in earlier to see him one last time. One RN stayed after her shift was over, because she had become very attached to Michael and she wanted to be there when he went home to the Lord. We patted Michael's hands and told him goodbye between our tears and pain. Our hearts were pierced and felt like they would break in two.

"Michael, let go. You're going to be with Jesus." We said the only comforting words we knew to our dear son.

Around eight o'clock that evening, tears streamed down Michael's face. Johnny used his handkerchief to wipe one side of his face and Martha wiped the other. Oh, the agony of seeing the line going straight on the screen. Oh, the pain of watching as the nurse pulled needles and tubes out of him, turned off monitors, and turned the machines backward so we would no longer see their painful blankness.

Again, my heart became so heavy that I thought it would break. *If only I could exchange places with him*, my heart cried out. Johnny wished for that also. But it was not to be. Then, about four minutes later, another set of tears ran down Michael's cheeks. Johnny and Martha did the same tender service, wiping his face, and then . . . he was gone. I looked up at the ceiling and waved to him, saying to myself, *Goodbye, my firstborn. We'll see you later. I hope the angels surround you until you come into the presence of the Lord.*

Just a few weeks earlier, I had read in a Billy Graham book about how the spirit hovers for a moment after death. My thoughts flew upward with him, precious memories of his life: how much he loved water and swimming but never liked darkness, how he loved our house dog, Coco, to greet him at night and run upstairs with him when he came home late.

Our hearts remained in that room even as our bodies took us out, down the hall, to the couch in the waiting room. Although it wasn't typical of Amish couples to do this in public, Johnny and I just clung to each other, holding each other, as we cried and cried. Turning to the only comfort we knew, I asked my brother-in-law John to find a Bible and turn to Psalm 46. He read, "God is our refuge and strength, a very present help in trouble" (Psalm 46:1). Those words penetrated my frantic thoughts. I clung to them during the chaotic days to come, repeating them to myself time and time again.

God carried us all the way through that dark time. He carried us during those long, anxious days while Michael was in the hospital. He carried us when the doctors came and said, "I'm sorry."

Michael died the night before Thanksgiving. What a Thanksgiving we had! When the funeral director brought his body to our house, to be placed in our new room for the viewing, he suggested we keep the casket closed because of Michael's terrible color. But we wouldn't hear of it. The viewing is a most important part of how the Amish pay their final respects, and we wanted that for him.

The funeral was held on Sunday. After the service, those gathered began filing past Michael's coffin to pay their last respects. Each one rose in order from their benches where they sat by age. On they came, past the coffin, into the kitchen, and out the door: friends and family, uncles and aunts, then brothers and sisters, until it was time for Father and Mother.

But I just couldn't go. I couldn't get off the bench. I knew that would be the last time I would see my precious son until we meet on the other side. People were waiting, but it felt like I was glued to the bench. Two or three times, I tried to stand, but my legs just did not move.

Johnny said gently, "Come on."

Finally, I stood and willed my legs to move toward that last moment with my son. When I finally looked at him, a piece of my heart ripped out of me and went into that coffin with him. It was the most heart-wrenching, painful experience of my life. It felt just like someone had taken a knife and twisted a piece of my heart out. Later when they screwed the coffin down, I had to hold my heart, it hurt so badly. Although time has dulled the pain, it is still there and will be with me until I die.

A few weeks later, Johnny had to go to Michael's bank to close his account. He had to sign many papers, but when the clerk stamped "Account Closed" it wrenched both their hearts. She and Johnny stood there crying. When Johnny came home and told me about closing the account and the fresh grief, he had to cry all over again.

Account Closed! We didn't have closure. We couldn't have closure until we found out what had really happened. We know from so many sources—more than you can imagine—that the official report of the accident isn't what actually happened. So many things happened that we couldn't understand—some very strange things. While he was still alive, the ICU received an anonymous call that said, "Watch Michael Miller, because someone might try to pull the plugs on him so he'll die." And reports from witnesses of the accident and the ambulance squad contradicted what the official report said. So we were still confounded with our grief and agony, and we also remained confused because the facts weren't adding up. We just couldn't put two and two together and make it come out four. Over the next several weeks and months we did our own investigation, and many unanswered questions remain in our minds about what happened that night.

———————————

Some people tried to console me after Michael's death by saying, "It was God's will." But I struggled with that. I just could not accept that this terrible thing that happened could be God's will. I had wrestled with this all those many days when I prayed in that hospital bathroom. Even as I finally prayed, "Thy will be done," I could not accept that this was God's perfect plan for Michael—to be taken from this life at such a young age.

Later I had to accept it and I did accept it, but it wasn't until years later when reading a devotional on the difference between God's perfect will and God's *permissive* will that I came to understand that not everything that happens is God's perfect will. His perfect will is unchangeable. But many things happen because of evil in the world, because of our choices, or because of reasons we may never know. I did find peace as I came to realize that God could turn even something so very tragic as losing my firstborn into his perfect will. He is our Redeemer, and he can redeem even the very worst in our lives.

In the weeks after Michael's funeral, some people told us of visions they'd had of Michael. Martha's mom said that before he died, the Lord revealed to her that Michael would be happy now and was smiling. Martha saw angels standing at the gravesite. Johnny's first cousin was lying in bed one night after the funeral when she saw her whole wall light up. Then she saw angels flapping their wings and rising into the air above Michael's grave.

Praise be to the Lord who was, and is, and is yet to come! Thank you for your mercy, poured out on us day and night. Amen. Lord Jesus, use me to point hearts toward the cross, where one glimpse will change everything for all eternity.

21

From Generation to Generation

LIFE WENT ON for us after Michael's death, but it was never the same. One person was missing at our table after Elizabeth got married, and now what a loss and big gap there was with Michael missing. It took weeks before the tears would quit when we all sat down to bow our heads and say our silent prayers.

The years following Michael's death held many important passages, including weddings of our children, births of our grandchildren and great-grandchildren, and a move for us into a doddy house (*Dawdy Haus*) next to our son-in-law Tim, daughter Esther, and their family, who had moved into the big house. When Tim and his family decided to leave the Amish church, our daughter Susan and her husband Jerry decided to buy the big farmhouse.

When we moved to our hundred-acre farm years before, we couldn't see another house but just our beautiful, rolling farmland. But now—after all the auctions and with all the children moving in and out and bringing in trailer houses and building homes—there are nine homes, one barn, a sawmill that has

The Miller farm in the summer of 2010. Johnny and Marlene's house is beside the pond. Their former house, where daughter Susan and her family live, is behind the barn.

been turned into storage units, and a few acres in the woods that someone else owns. Much blood, sweat, and tears—and many memories—are left all over those hundred acres.

There were also big and little disappointments along the way. Many of our children have left the Amish faith. This brought heartache, but Johnny and I knew that we had to let our children choose their own ways, even when we didn't agree. It seems that we still miss our children most at mealtime. They leave an empty spot at the table and an empty space in our hearts.

⊶━━━━━━━⊷

We had another scare when Matt was about fourteen. In our part of Ohio there is a lot of natural gas, and the gas company had a well on our hundred acres. The gas is drawn from the ground by a large pump, which has a big arm connected by belts and pulleys to a motor. Every day or so, a maintenance person from the gas company comes to monitor these pumps to make sure they are operating correctly.

Typically the area around a well or a pump is enclosed by a fence, but the well on our property did not have such a guard to keep kids and animals safe. Over the years, we had a couple of cows die from getting into a pump. When this happened, the gas company reimbursed us for our loss, and we didn't think much more about it.

One cool day, Matthew said to Elizabeth, "Hey Elizabeth, come and help me. The motor's running on one of those gas well pumps, but the arm isn't moving."

Elizabeth said, "Oh Matt, let it go until later."

But Matt didn't want to let it go, so he found another sibling and said, "The arm isn't pumping on that gas well out there, even though the motor is going."

"Don't worry about it. The man comes around every day or so to check the motor. He'll probably be by soon."

Those motors had a rhythmic sound as they pumped, and that noise was always in the background in our fields. Maybe that was what got Matt's attention—not hearing that familiar rhythm. When he looked back to where the pump was, he saw the reason. Being a young man, he thought, *I can fix it. I can just hook up those belts and get things going again.*

Elizabeth and Wayne were in the kitchen with me when we heard Matt screaming. We heard him in the basement, screaming. Then we heard him coming up the steps, still screaming.

Before we could even think to move, Matt reached the top of the stairs and stood right in the middle of the kitchen floor, screaming, "Help me, Mom!" Only it came out slurred and we hardly understood him.

We looked at him, trying to figure out what was wrong and how to help him. Matt was rocking back and forth, going from one leg to another, and staring into space.

"Help me, Mom. Help me, Mom." His speech was so slurred that it was almost impossible to understand.

"What has happened to you?" I asked.

He looked kind of dirty and out of it. There was no sign of the coat he had been wearing, and he was holding his arm.

"Why aren't you talking right?" I said.

At this he opened his mouth, and we saw that his tongue was split.

All our senses were alert, and I think he tried to say "gas well," but we couldn't make out the words.

Then Elizabeth saw blood running out his ear, and she said immediately, "We have got to get him to an emergency squad. Mom, you stay here. We'll take him to Winesburg to a squad." My children knew how I get overwrought during emergencies, and thought I would be less in the way and of greater help staying home with the other children.

Wayne and Elizabeth loaded Matt into Wayne's car and took him to Winesburg, where they alerted the firemen. The emergency workers immediately took him to the hospital in Massillon.

I called a driver and went to the hospital, where Johnny met us after someone notified him at work. When the doctor came out to talk to us after looking over Matt, he told us Matt's brain had been cut. While we were waiting, we tried to put two and two together to understand what had happened.

Meanwhile, somebody contacted the gas company, and a representative came right away to the hospital. Later, when we talked with the maintenance man who was in charge of the gas well on our property, he remembered driving up the road to that well. He saw Matt walk down over a hill, cross a ravine, and continue up the next hill. He particularly noticed that our dog Rusty was walking in front of Matt. This was odd, as Rusty, like most dogs, usually followed at our heels.

When the company man saw Matt, he thought, *What is that boy doing, coming from the direction of that well, with the dog out in front?* He went up to the well to check it and found Matt's coat.

Did that boy do something? he wondered. But no—there were three belts running three different pulleys to pump the gas out of the earth. After he heard about the accident, the gas man knew that the dog had been leading Matt home, right into the house.

Thinking back, we thought we had heard a muffled voice saying, "Help me, Mom," before Matt came into the basement. At this point, we began to get a picture of what had happened and understand the enormity of this accident.

Once Matt was awake, he remembered going to the gas pump and starting to work at putting the belts on the pulleys. He remembered getting two of the belts on and working on the third. There his memory stops.

The doctor helped us figure out what had happened. When Matt got the third belt on, that big pumping arm started moving, and his coat likely got caught in the pulley. It twisted him around and around until his head got slammed into the metal, cracking his skull. "You should have been dead right then and there," the doctor told Matt later. "If you had stayed lying there, you would have died."

They operated on him for about four hours and put in a plastic plate where his skull bone had been cut. The doctor told us they were using plastic instead of steel because they had found that people with steel plates got excruciating headaches in cold weather.

Matt was in the hospital about five days, and had to be put on antiseizure medication for a year. They said if they could keep him from having one seizure during that year, he would probably be okay for the rest of his life. It took another half year after that to wean him off the medication, cutting it down little by little, but he never had a seizure. Although we were pretty sure Matt had learned his lesson, we told him never again to think he could fix something on a gas well. I believe that even before Matt was home from the hospital, the gas company had put a fence around that gas well and a guard around all the belts and pulleys.

We'll always remember how at the hospital a doctor had repeated the benediction that had been pronounced at Matthew's birth. "Matthew, God has plans for you," the doctor said. "You should be dead with what happened to you."

We have had a lot of other losses along the way. Our son Stephen, who had so much trouble in adolescence, finally ended up in prison. Even prison hasn't seemed to help. My heart aches for him to turn to the Lord. He needs the Lord in his heart to help him change. Although Stephen was baptized with Matt when he was in his early twenties, I have always felt he joined church because he couldn't stand the fact that Matt was getting baptized. He had a competitive spirit, especially when his brother Matt was doing something. I also wondered if he thought that baptism would help change him; maybe he thought he would be a better person after he was baptized. But a personal relationship with the Lord is what we need to have a lasting change of heart. I always tell my grandkids and others in my family when they are getting baptized: "Baptism is not the answer to changing our hearts and our ways."

Another large grief struck when Johnny and the boys went into a business partnership with a man who cheated them. The business failed, and we ended up losing our farmland and our house in the process. Thankfully, our daughter Malinda and her husband Mark bought our house and the land, and we have been paying them back. This allowed us to stay in our home.

Having the business fail and losing our land and home was a difficult time for us, but through it all we never lost our faith in the Lord. We had been through many business reverses and had many trials, and losing our home was very hard. The Lord says we are to trust him for all our needs. That means we should approach a crisis with the assurance that God will bring

Marlene and Johnny's buggy and former horse, Nip, in their driveway.

good from it. God says in his Word, "I will never leave thee nor forsake thee" (Hebrews 13:5) and that we should only trust and obey. Johnny and I clung to these promises, holding on to our Lord. We knew that we would get through this time. Just as God had helped me through a dark time many years ago when I was overwhelmed, we would get through this. "Life will go on," we told ourselves. "It will get better."

One of the bright spots in my life has been becoming a member of a health supplement company and selling its nutritional powders and drinks. Since 2000, the products have helped me achieve better health and wellness, and I began counseling with other people, walking them through the steps toward better health. The results were contagious, as people started feeling better and having more energy. People sent friends and family members to me, and now it seemed I was running a health business besides doing all my own housework—cleaning, washing clothes, and canning. I never intended to have a health business; it just happened when I couldn't quit telling people about how much better I felt.

Working on the farm and watching our children grow put our lives into a pattern. There are so many milestones in a person's life: marriage, birth of a first child, children beginning school, finishing eighth grade, getting their first job away from home, first girlfriend or boyfriend. Johnny and I watched as many milestones came and went, not only in our lives but in the lives of our children.

It is amazing how life keeps going, generation after generation, for hundreds and hundreds of years. The Amish have existed for hundreds of years, and their songs and faith and traditions have been passed down. Time and events flow just like the waves of the ocean. They keep lapping against the shore, and it never ends.

A friend from my school days came to visit one day a few years ago. She was a majorette with me at Fairless High, and wanted to ask if I would march in the Fairless Alumni Band when the football season started again.

Needless to say, I nearly laughed myself off my chair onto the floor. I couldn't believe she was asking me to do this at my age. *No problem with the twirling,* I thought. So I said, "I can still twirl, but . . . I wouldn't think you would want an old Amish woman marching in front of the band wearing a dress instead of a uniform or shorts."

She said, "I don't care what you wear."

"Amish women wouldn't do anything like that," I nicely informed her. "That certainly wouldn't be allowed." She tried to convince me, but in the end she left.

As she was going, she said, "I'll be back in a couple more years; then maybe you'll change your mind." She did come back—three more times—to see if I had changed my mind.

The *Dawdy Haus,* where Marlene and Johnny live today.

I laughed at the thought, and told her no. Secretly, I was a little flattered.

All those years ago I did a 180-degree turnaround and have never regretted it. But I'm still the same when it comes to twirling. I still love to twirl for the strangers who come to visit the Amish woman who was called to be Amish. I love watching their faces and hearing how they laugh.

I still get together with some of my friends from my English life, especially the six girls from our Girls' Ensemble. I cherish their friendship even today. Ginny Bair Spidle always volunteers to take me to restaurants or to the latest outing. Several others also live nearby: Sherry Atkinson Hamner, Linda Fulton Hysong, and Kay Stutz Tucker. Cheryl Wohlheter Arthur ended up in Washington, and Ruth Moody lives in Michigan's Upper Peninsula. Another of my close friends is Miriam Harrold Cochran, who played in band and sang in chorus. I dearly loved those friends and still love it when we get together. They have absolutely no problem with the fact that I'm Amish. They can see, hear, and feel what Christ has done for me. Ginny cries when we talk, because she loves Jesus, too.

The current population of Amish in the United States is about 275,000. In *The Amish*, Donald Kraybill and his co-authors say that only about seventy-five outsiders have joined Amish churches—and remained members—since 1950. Just think how awesome God has been to me, and still is, in my life.

Every time I read about the apostle Paul, I relate to him more than to anyone else in the Bible. He was persecuting the Christians, but then he became blind and had to be led to a house, where he began a 180-degree turnaround in his life. That's how I feel about the turnaround in my life. Every time someone preaches about Paul, I perk right up. I love to hear about him, because I relate so much to his life. God has turned my life around, and I have walked worthy in the Lord, which is still my desire today.

I've read about Paul many times in my Bible and in my devotional books, especially about how his life was radically changed. The one I read recently, *Experiencing God Day-by-Day*, by Richard Blackaby and Henry Blackaby, states my exact sentiments at this time in my life:

> Because Paul's life had been radically transformed by the gospel, he was intent on living to honor the gospel that gave him life. It would have been disgraceful to be saved from death by the blood of Christ and then show no reverence for that sacrifice. It would have been foolish to accept such love from Christ and then to resent what He asked in return. The way a person lives his life ought to be a tribute to the matchless grace that our Lord and Savior, Jesus Christ, has bestowed upon us.

Entering a saving relationship with Christ is a life-changing experience. All things become new! Not some things—*all* things. Christ's presence in my heart gave me new thoughts, new attitudes, and more love and compassion. The dramatic changes that came into my life were initiated by God.

I was just an ordinary, nineteen-year-old former majorette. But the Lord wanted me to be Amish in order to accomplish things I'd never dreamed or imagined were possible. I could not have done it without the amazing grace of God, which saved a wretch like me. I was indeed lost and now am found; I was blind but now I see.

Lord Jesus, I praise you for being the "Author and Finisher" of my faith. May the grace and love of our Lord Jesus Christ be with you all. Amen.

A Day in the Life of the Author

Note: The following is a typical day in the life of the author after she had become Amish and while she and her husband were raising their young family.

STRAWBERRY SEASON: SUMMER 1980

4:30 a.m. Johnny wakes before the birds, but I still doze until 5:00. The children are awakened to help milk sixteen cows before he goes to his second job in a town nearby. After milking two or three cows, I hurry to the house to pack his bucket and prepare his breakfast.

7:00 a.m. All the chores in the barn are done and it's time for a breakfast of store-bought cereal, fresh strawberries, cake, or cookies. When the dishes are done and the floor swept, we head for the strawberry patch. We planted two thousand strawberry plants last year.

8:00 a.m. The children and I are picking like crazy! They'll pick until noon, but I'll have to leave at 10:00 or 10:30. I think they're eating more than what goes into the boxes. The sun is shining very brightly, so that means our oldest son has to stop picking and start raking hay. Hopefully we can put up hay when Dad comes home.

10:30 a.m. Time for me to go to the house and start lunch. Usually I make mashed potatoes, meat and gravy, vegetables, and applesauce, but today will be simple. The girls are bringing boxes and boxes of berries to stand on the cool floor by our water trough in the back basement. It keeps them colder there. I quickly do four quarts of berries for lunch.

12:00 noon It's late for lunch, as we almost always eat at 11:30. We only had fresh lettuce-and-lunchmeat sandwiches with potato chips, strawberries, cake, and fresh whipped cream.

1:00 p.m. Some of the children head for the patch again while the girls and I start cleaning and canning the berries. I add some strawberry gelatin to the sugared berries to make them redder, because if I don't, they'll turn pink. We will can fifty quarts, keep eight quarts for fresh, and then we will sell the rest of them by U.S. Highway 62, which is three miles from here. Daughter Susan usually gets that job.

4:00 p.m. Johnny is home. He and the boys start making hay. Supper will be after chores tonight. We have a basement kitchen, so we stay cooler in the summer. It consists of a long table, chairs, stoves, sink, and cupboards.

6:00 p.m. Because of haymaking, we're late for milking. The cows are giving more, too. The haymow and the barn smell so good with the first cutting of hay.

7:00 p.m. We're having our late supper. It consists of cold strawberry milk soup, trail-style bologna, Swiss cheese, and fresh onions and radishes.

10:00 p.m. After working hard all day, the children play badminton. Now it's finally time for baths. Always before we go to bed, we kneel down as a family to pray. Johnny reads a prayer out of our prayer book. It's been a very fruitful day—in more ways than one!

Marlene's Favorite Recipes

AMISH DRESSING

2 quarts bread cubes
3 eggs
enough milk to soak up all the bread, approx. 1 cup
salt and pepper to taste
¼ cup cooked diced carrots
1 cup cooked diced potatoes, salted
½ cup celery, finely cut
½ cup cooked, finely chopped chicken
1 cup broth

In a skillet, brown the bread cubes in butter. Turn often. Beat the eggs, add the milk and broth and salt and pepper, then mix in the rest of the ingredients. Add more milk, if needed, until the bread is well moistened. Put the mixture in a well-buttered baking casserole dish and bake at 350°F until brown all around, about 45 minutes. Or you can fry it in a skillet with some butter until brown.

SCRAPPLE

To make *Ponhaus*, or scrapple, we took broth from cooking meat bones, dumped the bones on a big butcher table, pulled the meat off and ground it, and put it back in the big iron kettle, which the men had simmering over a fire. Then I added whole-wheat flour or wheat germ, cornmeal, white flour, rolled oats, salt, and pepper. (The amount of ingredients depended on how many hogs we were butchering.) When it started bubbling (the men stirred it constantly or it would burn), we cooked it for 20 minutes and then ladled it into cake pans. This made a solid cake. We sold pans and pans of this. To eat it, you slice the cake, dust it with flour, and fry it in bacon grease until it gets crispy on the outside and a little soft on the inside. You must do this just right, or your husband won't like it. The Amish around here put apple butter on it and eat it for breakfast.

OLD-FASHIONED DATE PUDDING (Johnny's Favorite)

½ pound dried dates, chopped
2 tablespoons butter
1 teaspoon baking soda
1 cup boiling water
2 eggs
1 cup brown sugar; or half white, half brown
2 cups flour
1 teaspoon baking powder
½ teaspoon salt
½ cup chopped nuts

Mix together dates and butter. Add baking soda and pour boiling water over the mixture. Beat eggs and add sugar. Combine this mixture with the hot date mixture. Sift together flour, baking powder, and salt, and add to date mixture. Fold chopped nuts into the mixture. Pour into greased 9" x 13" baking dish and bake 40 minutes at 325°F. Finish with whipped cream on top. For a wedding or special occasion, garnish with half a maraschino cherry.

Johnny's mom would cut this cake into ½-inch cubes and layer it with real whipped cream, sweetened to taste, and slices of bananas.

POTATO DOUGHNUTS

2 cups mashed potatoes
3 tablespoons melted shortening
3 eggs
1 cup whole milk
5 cups flour
1½ cups sugar
5 teaspoons baking powder
1 teaspoon salt
¼ teaspoon nutmeg

Beat mashed potatoes, and add melted shortening, eggs, and milk. Sift dry ingredients together and add to liquids. Dough should be soft, yet firm enough to roll. Divide dough into four parts. Roll out one part at a time to ¾-inch thickness. Cut with doughnut cutter and drop into deep fat (375°F). Fry until golden-brown on both sides. (If a fat-frying thermometer is not available, test temperature of fat by dropping a ½-inch cube of bread into it. It should brown in one minute.)

Drain on absorbent paper. Shake in a paper bag containing white sugar and cinnamon, or powdered sugar. This makes approximately 4½ dozen doughnuts.

PUFFBALL OR QUICK TEA DOUGHNUTS
(Farmer's Buttons)

3 eggs
1 cup sugar
2 cups milk
½ teaspoon salt
2 teaspoons baking powder
2 cups flour
2 tablespoons melted fat

Beat eggs. Add sugar and milk. Sift dry ingredients together and add to liquid. Beat thoroughly and add melted fat.

Add more flour to make a batter stiff enough to hold a spoon in a standing position. Drop by spoonfuls into deep fat at 375°F. Remove when brown and drain on absorbent paper. This makes approximately 4 dozen.

DAMPF KNEPP
(Caramel Dumplings)

1 cup warm water
1 yeast cake (small) [equivalent to 2¼ teaspoons yeast, or
    1 packet]
1 egg
1 teaspoon salt
3 tablespoons sugar
1 tablespoon melted shortening
Flour (approximately 2½–3 cups)

Syrup:
3 cups water
2 cups brown sugar
1 tablespoon butter

Dissolve yeast in warm water. Beat egg and add sugar and salt. Combine yeast with egg mixture. Add flour and melted fat, and work into a smooth, soft dough. Turn out on a floured board and knead for several minutes. Place dough in a greased bowl and brush surface with melted shortening.

Cover and let rise in a warm place until double in bulk. Divide dough into six parts, work into smooth round balls, and let rise until light.

Place on top of boiling syrup. To make syrup, combine water, brown sugar, and butter, and cook together for 5 minutes. Cover and cook slowly, 25–30 minutes. Do not remove lid.

An old favorite of Grandmother's day. Raisins may be added to syrup if desired. Serves 6.

Author's Note: Don't peep in while the dumplings are steaming, as they will immediately start to fall. Everyone had to be at the table before I placed the pot there and took the lid off, because the dumplings looked so high, scrumptious, and mouth-watering. In individual bowls, place half a dumpling, fresh applesauce, and milk to cover.

The date pudding recipe is adapted from and the potato doughnuts, puffball doughnuts, and *Dampf Knepp* recipes are reprinted from Mary Emma Showalter, *Mennonite Community Cookbook, 65th anniv. ed. (1950; Harrisonburg, VA: Herald Press, 2015).* The *Mennonite Community Cookbook* has been reissued with new photography and is available from www.heraldpress.com or (800) 245-7894.

FAQs about the Amish: The Author Answers

Author Marlene C. Miller answers some frequently asked questions about Amish life, faith, and culture.

1. What kinds of prayers do the Amish say before meals?

Silent prayers. We teach the children when they're little what to pray for when we bow our heads.

2. Why don't the Amish evangelize?

We evangelize by example. We don't have a problem when other faiths do it. More people have come to us in Holmes, Wayne, and Tuscarawas Counties than we could have ever thought to evangelize elsewhere.

3. What do you think of Amish-themed fiction?

I don't think highly of it. It was told to me by a highly esteemed author that their publishers want more love scenes to make the books thicker. To me, they're dull and boring. I refuse to read them.

4. What do you think of Amish-themed television shows?

They're untrue and a disgrace. I watched about ten minutes of two different shows, and my jaw dropped in disbelief and I felt nauseated. I had to wonder what our God above thought of this trash!

5. How do you make sense of outsiders' intense interest in Amish life?

I can understand it, as I was always interested in their way, too. I had schoolmates who were Amish. They lived a peaceful and contented life—at least the majority of them did. The outsiders can have that same peace and joy without becoming Amish—just give the heart and soul over to Jesus.

6. Do the Amish pay taxes?

I can assure you that they do, and we do, too: real estate, income, and Social Security, if they work for English businesses. Of course, we get taxed at the pumps for gas, kerosene, and diesel for our engines. We even help pay for paved roads because the commissioners say that our buggy wheels make so many grooves in the roads.

7. Why do Amish children drop out in eighth grade?

They don't drop out; the parents make this decision. Who says higher education makes a person smarter and wiser? Does that really equip them for farming? We believe in hands-on education. Have people noticed that in this world, there are more trade schools than ever before? Holmes County, which contains the biggest Amish settlement in the United States, has one of the lowest unemployment rates in the country!

8. Do the Amish vote?

About half the Amish vote when an election is about local issues. But when it's for president, I'd guess only about one-quarter or so vote. That's more than it was fifty years ago.

The Author

MARLENE C. MILLER has been a member of the Old Order Amish church for forty-seven years. She grew up in a non-Amish home and during high school was a cheerleader and the head majorette. She and her husband, who was raised Amish, had three children before they were baptized. Marlene and Johnny have been married for fifty-one years and live on their farm in eastern Ohio. She is an AIM (American Image Marketing) International elite director and a "living well" coach. She and her husband have nine living children, forty-one living grandchildren, and ten great-grandchildren.